First Aid Kit for Teachers

Also available from Continuum

Getting the Buggers to Learn, Duncan Grey

Grey's Essential Miscellany for Teachers, Duncan Grey

Sue Cowley's Teaching Clinic, Sue Cowley

How to Survive Your First Year in Teaching, Sue Cowley

First Aid Kit for Teachers

Duncan Grey

continuum

Continuum International Publishing Group
The Tower Building   80 Maiden Lane, Suite 704
11 York Road   New York, NY 10038
London SE1 7NX

www.continuumbooks.com

British Library Cataloguing-in-Publication Data
A catalogue record for this book is available from the British Library.

ISBN 0826489621 (paperback)

Library of Congress Cataloging-in-Publication Data
A catalog record for this book is available from the Library of Congress.

Typeset by Data Standards Ltd, Frome, Somerset, UK.
Printed on acid-free paper in Great Britain by Ashford Colour Press, Gosport, Hampshire.

CONTENTS

LIST OF ACRONYMS AND ABBREVIATIONS

ACAS	Advisory, Conciliation and Arbitration Service
ADHD	Attention Deficit/Hyperactivity Disorder or Attention Deficit/Hyperactivity Syndrome
ALPS	Accelerated Learning in Primary Schools
ASD	Autistic Spectrum Disorders
ATL	Association of Teachers and Lecturers
BBFC	British Board of Film Classification
CMT or CIMT	Critical Incident Management Team
CPD	Continuing Professional Development
CRB UK	Criminal Records Bureau
CV	Curriculum Vitae
DfES	Department for Education and Science
DT or D&T	Design Technology
DVD	Digital Video Disk
EiC	Excellence In Cities
EOC	Equal Opportunities Commission
G&T	Gifted and talented
GCSE	General Certificate of Secondary Education
GTC	General Teaching Council
ICT	Information Communication Technology
INSET	In-Service Training
LA or LEA	Local Authority or Local Education Authority
LRC	Learning Resources Centre
NAS/UWT	The National Association of Schoolmasters Union of Women Teachers
NCSL	National College for School Leadership
NPQH	National Professional Qualification for Headship
NRT	National (Workforce) Remodelling Team
NUT	National Union of Teachers
OFSTED	Office for Standards in Education
PE	Physical Education
PPMR	preparation, planning, marking and recording
PSHE	Personal, Social and Health Education
QCA	Qualifications and Curriculum Authority
RE	Religious Education
SATS	Standardized Assessment Tasks
SENCO	Special Educational Needs Coordinator
TA	Teaching Assistant
TDA	Training and Development Agency for Schools
VLE	Virtual Learning Environment

PREFACE

The advice in this book comes from a great deal of personal experience and many mistakes as well as successes.

I have, regrettably, sometimes failed to follow some of this advice myself and I know not all the good advice will work well for you. If it did, teaching would be a much more formulaic process than it is. In fact, pupils, groups, teaching environments and teachers' skills and moods change so much that there can never be a perfect solution to teaching.

I hope *First Aid Kit for Teachers* is a book you'll turn to for help. What happens then is in your hands.

If you are a Head you may see references to teachers consulting the Head about problems. I hope that the advice in this book can be read as being for Heads too, in which case they will have to consult other Heads or their own advisers, or even the staff they work with. Everyone needs someone to talk to.

This book is something to be read in advance of these incidents so you are prepared. It's to be by your side, if you have a moment, to help you make decisions, if you're fortunate enough to have time. It's also there to compare notes and evaluate your own actions. Did you get it right? Did you avoid the worst traps? What did you forget to do?

Whatever you do, don't read this book as a warning to avoid teaching. If we followed the advice of some health and safety experts we might never get up in the morning. We might reflect that most deaths occur in bed, and that putting our socks on is statistically a hazardous procedure. Teaching remains a noble profession and having contact with pupils is stimulating and worthwhile. Don't let the risks and pitfalls put you off – but do go armed with the *First Aid Kit*.

So, off you go, ready to stand firm, take control and say with a steady voice, 'Calm down, everyone. Go back to your seats and get on with your work. It's all right, I'm a teacher.'

Duncan Grey
July 2006

PRINCIPLES OF *FIRST AID KIT FOR TEACHERS*

What is first aid?

First aid is the first assistance given before the arrival of a qualified expert.

It is knowledge about what to do if a problem arises.

It is also an accessible *reference* to try to avoid the problem in the first place.

The object of first aid

The object of first aid is to:

- stabilize a situation;
- prevent a situation becoming worse;
- promote recovery.

Format

Where possible the format of each entry is:

- Description;
- Cause;
- Action;
- Priorities;
- Alternatives;
- Avoid.

These headings echo the stages of medical first aid.

What equipment is needed?

First aid offers advice which generally does not require specialist equipment.

It could, however, benefit from a small, portable and easily assembled kit.

More than anything it requires a clear head and some common sense.

What makes this *First Aid Kit* useful?

Every teacher benefits from advice. Sometimes you walk into a situation where, as an adult professional among children and young people, you are expected to resolve the problem. If you don't, you could be accused of neglect. If you resolve it inappropriately, you could be accused of unprofessional behaviour. Non-teachers rarely appreciate how many personal interactions there are during a day – the vast majority of which are in public view and on which you will be judged.

First Aid Kit is sensible action for anyone who is on the spot when a problem occurs. It offers considered advice when you don't have the time to consider all the options. It tries to give helpful advice on preventing the problem getting worse and starting things on the road to recovery. It offers reassurance when everyone else is panicking. It may also cover your back.

Avoidance of problems and coping with them when they happen are professional skills. Make sure you are a member of an appropriate trade union or professional association. Keep up to date with the inevitable changes in your profession by reading professional journals, attending professional development opportunities and reading news and reports on websites.

And don't leave home without your *First Aid Kit*!

ESSENTIAL TEACHING METHODS

You can teach anything with this list of essential methods. It will take skill and experience to decide which method works best in each situation – will cooperation or competition produce the best result? – but it's a starting point.

You might even evaluate your past performance and consider whether one of the other methods might have worked better.

These fundamental teaching methods are here to remind you that pupils have preferences about the way they learn. And when they are taught the way they prefer to learn they generally behave better, enjoy themselves more and think of you and your school in a more positive way. These methods and the essential learning styles which follow may head off some of the problems listed in the body of this book, preventing a situation occurring in the first place. That is truly first aid for teachers.

Instruction

Although it may be true that 'I hear and I forget', some things do need to be told and accepted. Direct instruction still has its place. It conveys a lot of information quickly.

Instruction can be enhanced by note-taking and by subsequent active tasks to consolidate and test learning.

Example

Give an example relevant to the pupil's own experience where possible.

Appropriate examples make an idea relevant.

Our personal example, our attitude – whether helping, being patient, bad-tempered, harsh or caring – will directly influence our pupils too. We are all role models and it makes sense to be positive.

How you say something and how you yourself do it will last longer than what you say.

Analogy or comparison

Use simile and metaphor to describe things and to connect them to the pupil's experience.

Make ideas less abstract by comparing them with practical life.

Make meaningful comparisons between historical figures and modern personalities.

Provide two texts or two ideas for comparison. This generates more creativity than a single example. The examples can then serve as models for pupils' own work.

Experiment and discovery

Learning by doing is practical and creative. 'I do and I understand.'

It may take longer, but the learning lasts longer too.

The delight of discovering something for yourself can lead to a lifelong fascination. Plan to give time for children to do things for themselves under your guidance. These are learning opportunities and they are very valuable.

Collaboration

Working with someone else or in a small team gives many benefits which can last a lifetime. Sharing ideas and working cooperatively are skills much prized by industry and in our personal lives.

Competition

At other times competition between teams brings about a creative challenge.

Success is a great incentive and failure is a valuable lesson. There does need to be control to prevent the excesses of destructive 'bare-knuckle' competition.

Computer-mediated learning

Using a computer need not be a solitary activity. A computer can complement other activities and supply a team with additional powers and data.

Computers sprinkled liberally around learning areas are more likely to lead to balanced and practical use than if parked directly in front of each child. They are valuable tools, but not the only ones.

Mentoring

It's not only the teacher and teaching assistant who can give help and guidance. Older pupils listening to younger children reading aloud serve as an audience, and they learn about responsibility and caring in the process. Peer support groups countering bullying can be particularly effective. Older pupils organizing games and sporting or fund-raising activities learn important skills and become role models for younger pupils.

Building on prior learning

Knowing the starting point and previous experience of your learners will determine the content and the speed at which learning takes place.

Ask your pupils what they know, then start to add to it rather than landing them with new knowledge out of context. This is also a good time to find out their interests and enthusiasms.

Frameworks

Use scaffolding, writing frames and prompts to suggest an overall shape into which a pupil can slot their personal answer, or provide part of a pattern to which the pupils can add.

A framework could be a model, an incomplete shape or a template. It offers somewhere to start from and an example of a possible solution.

Later, the pupil can go it alone, but in the early stages a template banishes the tyranny of the blank A4 page.

LEARNING STYLES

As with the basic teaching methods above, appealing to pupils' preferred learning styles can help avoid the disruption caused by restless pupils.

We all learn in our own unique way, with our own preferences. Where one child prefers to talk and write, another will prefer to explore and build; one focuses alone while another is inspired by working with others. Learning styles are not what we learn but how we learn.

This is not an argument for appealing *only* to each child's preferred learning style. That would reinforce the preference and discourage the development of alternative learning methods which might help the learner. Nor does it mean entirely individualized learning for your 30+ pupils!

What it does mean is that by recognizing learning preferences you can offer a range of ways for children to learn; different routes for reaching a common goal. In addition we can provide activities which will develop each child's range of learning methods in order to enhance effective learning.

We might suggest four ways of presenting their research information or offer a choice that they either write a fact sheet or prepare and deliver a talk. We could vary group work to allow members of a team to contribute according to their strengths and take different roles from time to time.

The identification of seven learning styles is simply a convenience. There can be as many as you like, but the following seven are based on the work of Gardner and Hatch (1989) and have been enthusiastically taken up by accelerated learning programmes. The number, terminology and definitions may change but the idea remains the same – take into account pupils' preferred learning styles and both behaviour and learning will improve. That is truly personalized learning.

Seven learning styles
Physical learners
They fidget and can't sit still. They think better when they are moving. They enjoy sports, dancing and making things. They gain from role-play, movement exercises and touching things.

They often enjoy performing and could become dancers, athletes, surgeons or craftspeople.

Intrapersonal learners
They are loners and may be shy and thoughtful. They aren't necessarily antisocial, but think better on their own, independently and reflectively.

They enjoy writing journals and diaries and exploring the Internet. They gain most from self-paced activities, independent projects and research.

They could become psychologists, novelists or computer programmers.

Interpersonal learners

They are sociable, helpers and team players. They like to interact with others and share ideas. They understand how people work together.

They enjoy team sports and group discussions, playing cooperative games, researching with partners or working in small groups.

They could become counsellors, teachers, politicians, entertainers or go into public relations.

Linguistic learners

They enjoy words, and learn through language. They express themselves through speech and writing.

They enjoy giving speeches, writing poetry and reading. They learn through storytelling, listening to lectures, taking part in interviews and by reading and writing.

They could become authors, journalists or lecturers.

Mathematical learners

They enjoy games, maths puzzles and rule-based activities. They think in logical ways, though they may not be neat and orderly. They relate through reasoning, numbers and patterns.

They enjoy counting, making timelines and solving puzzles.

They learn through performing scientific experiments, following step-by-step processes and using calculations.

They could become scientists, accountants, engineers or lawyers.

Musical learners

They enjoy humming, singing and tapping. They are not necessarily the best singers or musicians, but they respond to melody, rhythm and sound. They enjoy listening to songs, playing instruments and singing.

They learn by writing song lyrics, playing music with their work or developing multimedia projects.

They may become singers, musicians, orchestra conductors, recording engineers or Web designers.

Visual learners

They doodle, draw and enjoy colour. They have an artistic sense and relate through pictures and images. They enjoy painting, sculpting and creating graphs.

They learn by drawing diagrams, reading flowcharts, creating maps or designing visual Web pages.

They may become architects, pilots, designers, painters or sculptors.

If you find that more than one learning style applies to you, then this may make you a more varied learner. If you prefer one learning style for some activities and a second or third for other activities, then you are likely to be a skilled learner who can make a conscious choice of the most effective style for the task.

This is what we should be aiming for with our pupils – to make them effective learners with a range of learning strategies at their fingertips.

That this may avoid some of the behavioural problems addressed in this book is a further great advantage of having effective and satisfied learners.

The Steer Report on behaviour notes: 'It is recognized that the most common forms of misbehaviour are incessant chatter, calling out, inattention and other forms of nuisance that irritate staff and interrupt learning.'

This is precisely the sort of underlying disruption which can be reduced by choosing appropriate teaching and learning methods.

WHOLE-SCHOOL CRITICAL INCIDENTS

Critical incidents are defined as:

> Unexpected occurrences which may suddenly have a major impact on school on a scale beyond the coping capacity of the school operating under normal conditions.

A critical incident may be:

- an arson attack or major fire;
- a pupil suicide or sudden death;
- the sudden tragic death of member of staff;
- a violent attack on a member of the school;
- an armed or violent intruder on school premises;
- a road traffic accident, with school fatalities;
- an abduction or disappearance;
- allegations or actual incidents of abuse;
- any incident causing sudden school closure.

Preparation

Preparation is the best way to minimize the effects of a critical incident. This is an outline summary but your list must be complete, thorough, should conform to Local Authority (LA) policy, be approved by emergency services, rehearsed and evaluated.

Team

Create a Critical Incident Management Team (CIMT).
Make sure this team is known to all staff and governors.

Plan

Design a plan to suit your school.
Include a strategy for communicating, for making areas of the school private, providing classroom support and counselling, an instant assembly to occupy pupils while their teachers are involved in the incident.
Create an incident log to record what should be done and what is actually done in the event of an incident.

Identify and describe

Identify the range of crises or incidents that could affect your school. This is the basis for a risk assessment.

Base

Establish a base from which the CIMT can operate, with appropriate facilities to contact pupils, teachers, parents, LA support services and education officers, counsellors, the media. Also identify a separate back-up base.

Communication

Ensure that, in the event of a critical incident, the CIMT can communicate with each other, emergency services, members of the school community and the wider community.

Consider mobile phones, phone landlines, radios, text messaging, laptops with a variety of potential connections (network, wireless, dialup modem, broadband). Don't forget posters and news bulletins at the school gates and usual parking places.

Create an essential phone list, list of contact names and a telephone tree.

Identify and publicize rendezvous points, sources of further information (local radio, school website, recorded message, phone contact number).

Grab bag

Identify an essential kit for guarding in the event of fire or using to set up the CIMT base. Make sure this will be packed, ready and retrieved in any emergency.

Checklist of constantly updated information

This could be available online at a distant location, on a local back-up disk or on a laptop, but must be available, safe and up to date. The list should include:

- contact details of pupils and staff, governors, key holders;
- LA emergency contact numbers;
- bus/coach lists;
- emergency supply/support list;
- information sheet about the school providing basic details;
- site plan;
- timetables and registration data – who is where, including off-site details;
- list of school first-aiders;
- list of high-risk pupils;
- school bank details;
- copies and location of keys;
- back-up disks for all accounts.

PART 1 DISCIPLINE AND BEHAVIOUR

Low-level disruption is a more pervasive problem than outright refusal or violence.

School rules are usually very clear about absolute criteria, but only experience and professionalism from the teacher and the ethos of the school can cope with the energy-sapping attempts by pupils to ignore requests, act deaf to instructions, reel off excuses or do the minimum of work.

1 SCHOOL RULES AND EXPECTATIONS

They don't obey the school rules.

Description

School rules must be laid out clearly and agreed by all parties – teachers, pupils, school management, parents, governors, local authority.

You should know where to find these rules and make it a responsibility to bring them to the attention of pupils. This is too often done when pupils enter the school, then left and forgotten.

Causes

Laying down rules requires strictness and consistency, yet implementation requires sensitivity and flexibility. It is this uneasy line that teachers defend hour by hour while pupils attack any weakness.

Meanwhile the practical expectations that the school has for its pupils and its teachers may not be so formally agreed – and even if they are, the expectations in the corridors and the classrooms may differ substantially from what is written and may vary between teachers.

All this causes a dislocation between theory and practice, the written rules and the rules on the ground. If white trainers are forbidden, what do we do about mainly black with white flashes? And how big can those flashes be? The school must together decide, explain, justify and make the decision and the penalty for disobedience clear. Individual teachers trying to stem the tide soon give up in the face of sullen lack of cooperation.

Incidentally, pupils seem to learn the informal rules of the school quickly by osmosis, though some of the formal rules and their language may not even be understood.

Distinguishing between given rules and actual expectations can be troublesome, especially for a new teacher. To reprimand a boy for walking on the right instead of the left might be seen as pedantic or even bewildering where it contradicts custom and practice.

Action

If you are new to a school, take time to look, listen and learn from teachers and pupils alike.

Share a duty with another teacher to judge when to act, when to punish, when to be stern and when to look the other way.

Priorities

Expectations in public areas are much more difficult to police and to judge than in your own classroom. You must impose standards of behaviour, of work or of silence on the pupils in your care. Consistency is usually appreciated in the long run and in your classroom you can maintain a standard. Imposing standards of behaviour on a mass of pupils milling about in a common area is much more difficult for a single teacher to achieve. In this we must all work together.

Following up misbehaviour is important. Ensuring that a fair punishment is served and that you mean what you say is essential.

One way that the school can assure itself that rules are known and agreed to is by using a code of conduct and an agreement signed by school, parents and pupils. This formalizes the rules, gives all parties the opportunity to object while the situation is calm and is proof of agreement if rules are broken. Even if it is not a legal document it is a strong token.

Alternatives

Remember that fairness is appreciated more than strict adherence to rules, but it is far more difficult to achieve. A reasonable attitude with a small degree of flexibility, an iron fist in a velvet glove, is likely to work best.

Avoid

A strident enforcement of minor infringements. The 'zero-tolerance' model may work in a society which wields guns and batons, but doesn't help in a school community where learning is a priority.

2. BULLYING (OF AND BY PUPILS) – PREVENTION AND AVOIDANCE

I suspect a child in my class is being bullied but I haven't seen anything I can deal with.

Description

Typical bullying behaviour towards others is usually easy enough to explain:

> If your behaviour makes someone else unhappy, uneasy or fearful, it is unacceptable. It makes no difference that you didn't know it upset someone. If it disturbs someone else, don't do it. Similarly, if your behaviour makes life more difficult for others or disturbs the learning of others then it is unacceptable. If by your behaviour other people suffer, or property is lost, stolen or damaged, that is unacceptable. The school will not accept that, teachers will not accept that and society will not accept that.

What is more difficult is identifying cases of bullying in the first place. Bullies are generally cunning and clandestine in their activities, even to the extent of getting others to do the bullying for them.

Also there are degrees of bullying, including subtle undermining over a long time.

Cause

Bullies are often insecure and insensitive, taking strength from the ability to dominate others and the apparent respect they get from others. Often the victim is unaware of the reasons for being picked out. In a small number of cases they even seem to collude with the bully in order to gain a kind of friendship.

Although some children seem to stand out as perpetual victims through some perceived or actual weakness, this is not a justification for failing to prevent the bullying.

The first aid approach is generally to put aside the causes and address the actions directly. Treat the causes later when things have calmed down, when there are others to advise you and there is more background to draw on.

Action

Pupils may need to have the consequences of their actions explained to them. They may not realize that name-calling is a form of bullying, or that swearing is frightening and can be racist or sexist. They may not realize that hanging around in large groups is intimidating. Differences of culture, religion, age and gender can cause genuine misunderstanding in language and behaviour. Pupils may need to be taught this explicitly.

Priorities

The main priority is of course to put a stop to the bullying. A teacher charging in may help in the short term but on its own this is unlikely to stop the problem long term.

So, a priority must be identification of the problem leading to realization of its importance by the pupils. This is a pastoral issue and one which requires explanation if pupils are to fully realize the effect they have on others.

Explain that what seems to be acceptable among adolescent white male friends may be entirely unacceptable to a young Muslim woman, an old man or a physically disadvantaged person. It may even be hurting people in their own group who don't complain in order to keep the peace.

If that doesn't sink in, punishment of the bully is almost inevitable.

Alternatives

Role-play enacting common bullying circumstances has been shown to help bullies understand the significance of their actions.

A Peer Support Group supervised by teachers can be an excellent forum for identifying and openly discussing bullying.

Avoid

Simply imposing rules. Explain them in clear terms.

Do not accept the commonest reasons given by pupils behaving badly:

- 'I didn't know.'
- 'I didn't do anything.'
- 'It was just a laugh.'

3 RACISM

I overheard a pupil describe another in racist language. What should I do?

Description

Racism is a particular kind of bullying. In most cases treat a racist incident as a bullying incident. Racism is the belief that some 'races' are superior to others and prejudice frequently targets skin colour or other physical characteristics.

Cause

Fundamentally this is a lack of understanding about another group of people. Prejudices build up, inequalities are perceived and certain features are attributed to a particular group. This in turn distances the groups from each other and increases the lack of understanding.

Action

Take what pupils are telling you very seriously.

Make sure you record, report and take action on racist incidents.

Remember that some pupils experience racism outside school all the time. Racist graffiti, name-calling and intimidation may be part of their school journeys and their daily life.

Celebrate diversity. Respect different cultures.

Ensure this is enshrined in a school policy.

Priorities

Make sure that pupils know you will not tolerate racism or bullying and that you will always deal with it.

Ensure pupils feel safe, valued and respected in school.

Make sure all pupils understand that abusive language can hurt as much as physical abuse.

Make clear that punishment or suspension are inevitable if this continues.

Make clear that racist bullying is against the law.

Alternatives

Build in an appreciation of diversity into all areas of the curriculum. Challenge stereotypes and prejudice in drama and Personal, Social and Health Education (PSHE), discuss etymology and connotations of language in English; discuss notions of empire, slavery and identity in History, Geography and RE; shuffle group membership and teams in all subjects.

Hold an assembly to make sure your message reaches everyone. Invite community members too.

Avoid

Turning a blind eye to any racist incident. Always take action when an incident occurs.

4 BULLYING (OF AND BY STAFF) – PREVENTION AND AVOIDANCE

I'm being dominated, disparaged and undermined by a senior colleague.

Description

Teachers as well as pupils can be bullies or be bullied. Indeed teachers are the largest professional group to contact the Bully Online website.

Bullying is: 'the unjust exercise of power of one individual over another by the use of means intended to humiliate, frighten, denigrate or injure the victim' (NAS/UWT, 1996).

The Protection from Harassment Act 1997 makes harassment both a civil tort and a criminal offence.

Harassment, in general terms, is

> unwanted conduct affecting the dignity of men and women in the workplace. It may be related to age, sex, race, disability, religion, nationality or any personal characteristic of the individual, and may be persistent or an isolated incident. The key is that the actions or comments are viewed as demeaning and unacceptable to the recipient.

Workplace bullies can be publicly dismissive and privately scornful, causing serious loss of confidence in the victim, leading to errors which are in turn criticized.

Classroom teachers are in the perfect position to be bullies and may rationalize picking on certain pupils 'for their own good'. Heads and deputies may have a similar attitude to their staff, targeting a young sensitive teacher or an older teacher approaching retirement and imposing their experience and personality in the cause of efficiency or professional standards.

Cause

One cause is the dislocation between older teachers who joined a traditional and largely unsupervised profession and more recent teachers used to the imposition of curriculum, assessment, management and supervision in the name of accountability.

Another cause is a combination of the bully's personality and their success in getting their own way by trampling on others. Pressure on school management to meet targets, balance budgets and improve performance can appear to them as dynamic strength but to others as ruthless and heartless efficiency.

In the victim, resentment of criticism builds into antagonism which can turn inwards and cause illness.

Action

Record all incidents in as dispassionate a way as possible, including quotation, date and background. Public incidents involving humiliation, dressing down, unfavourable comparisons with other staff, personal criticisms, rudeness and abuse should include an incident report from witnesses.

However, remember that fair criticism, however painful for the individual, is not bullying. Ask unbiased witnesses their opinion and listen carefully to their answers. If they have further personal examples, collect them too.

Contact your union, ask for advice and read their publications dealing with harassment in the work place.

Read your school's bullying/harassment/grievances policies.

Read publications by the Advisory Conciliation and Arbitration Service (ACAS), Equal Opportunities Commission, Commission for Racial Equality, Disability Rights Commission, as appropriate.

Arrange an appointment with the bully, accompanied by your union representative or a colleague. Present your grievance and ask for an explanation. Make notes of the responses. It's possible that this meeting will solve the issue simply by making the bully aware that there is a problem.

Visit www.bullyonline.org/workbully/teachers.htm

Priorities

Take action sooner rather than later. Do something, don't suffer.

Persist until the problem is resolved.

Get the matter into perspective by talking it over with other professionals and your union.

Follow the established procedures of your school, local authority or union.

Alternatives

Pay scrupulous attention to your performance – in the classroom and around the school. Ensure your personal appearance, demeanour and overall professionalism are impeccable. Not only will this make you feel more confident (though it will be stressful) but you should be unimpeachable. If bullying continues despite this, you will be in an even stronger position when you finally present your grievances.

Counselling can provide a release for your stress and a route to resolve the complaint. Counselling should be seen as a positive decision to solve a problem, not a sign of weakness.

Avoid

Becoming ill through worry. Taking action will cause some stress but relieves stress overall and eventually.

Leaving your job with the problem unsolved. The issue will remain with you and others will have to face the same problem.

5 DISRUPTIVE BEHAVIOUR – PREVENTION AND AVOIDANCE

A small number of pupils are disrupting my class so much I can't teach.

Description

Behaviour which disrupts the learning of others is always unacceptable. Explaining this to the whole class emphasizes the effect the pupil is having on his or her peers as well as on the teacher. Low-level disruption is difficult to clamp down on without seeming petty; however it can lead to greater disruption if left unchecked.

Cause

The causes of bad behaviour are many and various. The first aid approach is generally to put aside the causes and address the actions directly. Tackle the immediate actions and criticize or warn against them, avoiding criticism of the person. Treat the causes later when things have calmed down, when there are others to advise you and there is more background to draw on. In the meantime appreciate that though you may be the immediate focus for their anger you are probably not the real cause of it.

Action

Inappropriate behaviour in lessons, which leads to disruption of the learning of others, is entirely unacceptable and should be dealt with promptly and firmly. Deal with the behaviour, not the character of the child.

This may need reinforcement of classroom rules such as no calling out, no walking around the room, refusal to accept swearing.

Target those who seem to be causing the disruption directly. Don't blame the whole class for the bad behaviour of a few.

Where possible, adopt a considered form of words such as: 'Are you refusing my reasonable request to obey school rules?' This clarifies the situation and strengthens your position.

Prefer the word 'unacceptable' to 'bad'. Trying to convince a child that this or that is 'not acceptable' seems to me easier and less emotionally loaded than the morality of good and bad.

Move seating so that disruptive pupils are less likely to interfere with others.

Remove equipment from the pupil if it is being used as part of the disruption but clearly explain that it will be returned in time.

Repeated or severe disruption may require removal of a pupil. Make sure you know the procedure for this (check school rules), how to alert senior colleagues, whether there is a supervised cooling-down room.

If a pupil refuses to leave the room, a colleague may be able to save the situation because the pupil is not losing face by submitting to you.

In extremis, consider removing the whole of the rest of the class, leaving the problem pupil alone in the room.

Priorities

Resumption of normal learning for all pupils.

Keep an appearance of calm even if you don't feel it. The pupil is wrong, you are right. Stay in control for the good of the rest of the class. Most of the remaining pupils will appreciate this – though they are unlikely to show it.

Alternatives

Change activities and consider excluding the disruptive pupil from them.

Praise other, well-behaved pupils for their good behaviour and positive participation.

Implement a '3 strikes and you're out' policy across the school. Some schools have a scheme where a yellow card is given out for unacceptable behaviour and three cards lead to a detention. Notably good behaviour can lead to a card being withdrawn.

House points, class behaviour stars and similar schemes utilize peer pressure to improve individual and collective behaviour; however these are unlikely to be effective with older pupils.

The most likely children to be suspended according to DfES figures are boys aged 13 and 14. While it is neither an excuse nor a solution, it might help to remember that they are the victims of their own hormones.

Avoid

Physical confrontation.

Answering back in kind.

Blaming the pupil's character or background.

Becoming over-emotional. However, you may need a break after the incident to compose yourself.

6 RESPONSIBILITY AND PRIVILEGE

You can't do that – I know my rights.

Description

Being a member of any society brings with it certain responsibilities, which can in turn lead to privileges. It is society's bargain that privileges are appreciated because they are earned, and that people avoid being irresponsible because that means loss of privileges.

That bargain needs to be explained and made clear. It seems entirely just that pupils who don't look after the classroom are excluded from it at lunchtime and break, or that unacceptable behaviour in public means you cannot attend a social activity or treat.

Where this becomes more of a problem is where large numbers are involved and where innocent or well-behaved pupils have privileges withdrawn through the bad behaviour of others. It is generally agreed that, despite the convenience and power of peer pressure, it is not good practice for innocent members of a class to be made to suffer for the faults of others. Nevertheless if individuals can't be identified, the whole group may ultimately have to suffer.

Cause

Why would some pupils ruin their own classroom, block up their own toilets and damage the plants and trees around their school?

They may have a grudge against society, feel downtrodden, unappreciated, embittered and undervalued. It may be a product of thoughtlessness and a lack of appreciation of their privileges. It may be that they don't know the difference between a right and a privilege and they take their privileges for granted. It may simply be that group dynamics and hormones take over and they follow the crowd, doing things they would never consider on their own and for which they have no explanation. Maybe they don't understand their behaviour any more than you do!

Action

Explaining well before any incidents or confrontations that privileges rely upon responsibility and can be withdrawn is important groundwork. Indeed showing that certain things pupils think are their rights are in fact earned privileges can be a salutary lesson. Reinforcing that message following an incident is also valuable.

Warning of withdrawal of privileges is also important in advance of a possible incident:

> Anyone who fails to finish this work by next Friday will be unable to watch the film the following week.

> Anyone found with an alcoholic drink will be sent home immediately.

Priorities

Prompt action demonstrates that you consider this is important.

Preventing a recurrence is important.

Prompt maintenance sends a signal that a clean and tidy environment is high on your list of priorities. Attending quickly to small graffiti and damage limits its spread.

Alternatives

Clearly and patiently warn and explain that there are inevitable consequences to unacceptable behaviour.

Avoid

Where possible, withdrawing privileges without warning.

Overdoing the appearance of bribery.

Making the innocent suffer in order to put pressure on the troublemakers.

7 KNOWING PUPILS

You boy, what's your name, come over here.

Description

Cultivating a conscious habit of learning names of pupils and remembering significant things about them can save you time, embarrassment and help you solve a wide range of problems.

Cause

It is a real problem in large secondary schools, particularly if you teach a subject to a large number of classes only once or twice a week.

Superficially, knowing names means you can identify troublemakers and avoid being taken for a ride by a new class: 'He's not called Wayne, Miss, I'm called Wayne, Miss.' 'We're all called Wayne, Miss!'

More significantly, it means you can build better relationships with a wider range of pupils. You can also write more informed reports and speak meaningfully about personalities and achievements at parents' evenings. Not knowing names of pupils you teach says, 'I don't know you and you don't matter.' Knowing your pupils is a professional skill which can lead on to real understanding.

Action

Make time for deliberate practice of learning names in the classroom.

Use name cards on desks, make it into a game, do some research on the origin and meanings of their names. Explain this as a good example of learning in action. Your pupils can use these activities to learn their own work.

Force yourself to use names instead of pointing. Anything to build up your data bank.

In the classroom, use a seating plan (or several if you teach in different rooms) and insist it is adhered to.

Priorities

Know your pupils. It's a professional essential.

Alternatives

If you have difficulties remembering names, I sympathize. A tactic I used is to obtain or make a class list and annotate it with descriptions, incidents and comments. If you can obtain a class list with photographs from your school management system before the start of the year, get your family and friends to test you before you even enter school. If necessary take a photograph of the class in the first lesson and annotate it.

Avoid

Avoid picking on a pupil just because you know his/her name.

And don't use your knowledge of a pupil or their family to embarrass them in public. Don't compare a child to his/her brother or sister – or his/her parent, if you've been around that long!

8 KNOWING PUPILS TOO WELL

He touched me . . . .

Description

From time to time pupils get overfamiliar with their teacher. Also from time to time teachers have inappropriate feelings for pupils.

The teacher represents authority and high standards as well as caring for their welfare. The UK Criminal Records Bureau (CRB) check is intended to ensure that teachers have no record of inappropriate behaviour towards pupils. List 99, held by the Department for Education and Science (DfES), records all those who are banned from working with children.

Cause

Caring for the welfare of your pupils is a good thing – but over-familiarity which exceeds professionalism must be avoided.

Adolescent pupils in particular need saving from their own emotions and may be uncertain about standards of dress and behaviour. They may react irrationally and unpredictably.

Teachers of a certain age should not mistake familiarity for fondness and must not be drawn into an inappropriate relationship.

Action

Keep your distance. You are there to teach and educate. If you become an untrained counsellor or confidant you risk treading on the wrong side of a very fine line. This is sad but true and the consequences can be disastrous.

Young children who are upset may really need a cuddle, but male teachers giving hugs to female pupils run a serious risk in today's sensitive climate.

Keep your door open when talking one-to-one with pupils.

Have another responsible adult with you when talking to individual vulnerable pupils.

Record conversations and meetings and make them available, showing that you are open about meetings. If this could prejudice confidentiality, it is a fine judgement, but a small price to pay for avoiding accusations.

Priorities

Keep a professional distance.

Remember you're primarily a teacher, not an uncle, aunt or friend.

Remember that children are vulnerable emotionally and that you are a responsible adult. They are in your care, *in loco parentis*, and you must behave responsibly – even if they don't.

This doesn't mean you should avoid issues that would help the child, but consider that they may be better dealt with elsewhere and by others.

Alternatives

Refer delicate situations to counsellors and take no further part.

Consider the point of view of the parents.

Avoid

Compromising situations such as being alone with a child or touching a child.

Any suggestion of an emotional or physical relationship outside school is strictly off limits.

9 PRAISE V. CRITICISM

I want to say, 'Well done everyone . . .' but it sounds rather empty.

Description

Deserved praise is an incentive, deserved criticism can be an incentive. Undeserved praise does no one any good and undeserved criticism can cause very negative reactions.

But who says it's deserved or not? The teacher is in the hot seat and should sometimes expect to argue his/her case against a hurt pupil.

Cause

Criticism stings and stays with us. It can be hurtful and long lasting, even if the criticism is made out of a desire to help. Praise can buoy us up and make us give of our best. It's a curious thing that teachers, who should be looking for opportunities to give praise and emphasize the positive, are particularly bad at praising each other.

None of this is to go to the extreme of ensuring no one is criticized and no one should fail. We have to be realistic, and as Quakers say, 'There is that of good in every man' – it's just that the thirtieth exercise book may feel like one too many, and the umpteenth pupil may have hidden their goodness so deeply as to make it invisible.

Action

Aim to praise twice as much as you criticize, but don't overdo public praise if pupils are likely to be embarrassed or viewed negatively as goody-goodies.

Criticize the behaviour, not the pupil's character. If behaviour is inappropriate, say so – but don't assume it's because of some moral failing by the child. There may be background reasons you know nothing about.

Give the pupil the opportunity to grow up. While it's natural to bear in mind previous misbehaviour, how is the child to get a chance to start again if you have already made up your mind about him/her?

Priorities

Aim to praise more than you criticize.

Look for opportunities to praise even where there are obvious things to criticize.

Make criticism positive – 'This sentence isn't very effective. But if you try splitting it up and using a conjunction it could be really good.'

Avoid

Try to avoid taking out your bad temper on pupils.

Be prepared to admit you're grumpy, and apologize if necessary.

10 MUTUAL RESPECT

How do I get pupils to respect me as a teacher?

Description

Mutual respect is a marvellous aim. It comes from being honest, fair, firm and consistent. In a community such as a school it means everyone will recognize the strengths and weaknesses of each other and get on together.

If that sounds saintly I suppose it is, but it is worth working towards because one way or another you are a role model.

Cause

Lack of respect may come from children's expectations of other teachers or from knowing you. Respect is hard to gain and easy to lose.

Action

Aim to be honest, fair, firm and consistent with pupils.

Listen and try to understand the other person and their point of view. This doesn't mean that you have to agree with them, however.

Bolster this with high standards and a fundamental baseline of right and wrong.

Be friendly but firm, and remember you're a teacher, not a friend.

Alternatives

In the novel *To Sir with Love* by E. R. Braithwaite the aspiring young teacher eventually wins the respect of his class by defeating the tough pupil in a boxing match. This option is unlikely to be open to you – was it ever? – but showing you *genuinely* are interested in your pupils and the topics which are important to them (but not *pretending* to like their music and youth culture) can do no harm and may help your mutual relationship.

If pupils become aware that you are an interesting person in your own right, they are more likely to treat you with respect than if they see you as 'just' a teacher.

Avoid

Don't overdo the 'I feel your pain' attitude or make out you're a cool dude underneath your ageing exterior. You may not notice but they'll see right through you.

11 CLASSROOM ROUTINES

Sometimes I just can't be bothered to insist my class puts away coats and bags. It seems more bother than it's worth!

Description

Routines are important. They simplify life and take out the effort of decision-making – and therefore of arguing. Which sock and which trouser leg do you put on first when you dress? It's a routine you can follow even half asleep. The same can be said of the classroom. If the class always takes off coats, puts bags away, gets materials ready at the start of a lesson, there is no point in them arguing about it. If a particularly awkward pupil does argue, they must know they won't get anywhere.

None of this is to say that your *lessons* will be unvarying in their method, sequence or content. The routine is a kind of bookend that ensures the content is suitably framed. Like the theme tune of a soap opera it starts and finishes predictably, though what goes on within may vary.

Cause

A pupil who does argue or defies you will know they are doing so against a background of accepted routine. They are already losing when you point out that it's perfectly reasonable, everyone else does it and that's just the way it is.

Breaking the routine should not be done lightly, if ever. You have the class in the palm of your hand because they are following a pattern you have laid down for them.

Action

As you start your career, decide on the routines you are going to hold to. If it's routine for you as well as your pupils, it's easier for everyone.

Ensuring silence at the beginning and end of a lesson is vital, as it is during a roll call.

I advocate starting the roll call again from the beginning if there is any disturbance or noise to interrupt it.

Choose from the following routines, for example:

- *Entering the classroom* – how and when they enter, sit, unpack, prepare, become quiet, begin a starter activity
- *Bags, phones, equipment* – what's acceptable and what is not, dealing with lack of pens or pencils
- *Calling the register* – formal or informal, recording absence, allowing for absence
- *Handing out work* – monitors, collection, calling out names, making your comments, dealing with absence
- *Collecting in work* – monitors, on your desk as they leave, dealing with homework not done, dealing with absence
- *Packing up, tidying up* – leaving adequate time before the end of the lesson,

ensuring the room is tidy, arrangements for seeing individual pupils if necessary. Prevent pupils packing up too early. Ensure they leave in good order, for example by rows or columns according to which is sitting up straightest or by tables according to who worked hardest today.

Priorities

Adoption of a set of unvarying routines.

Silence and attention at start and end of lessons.

Alternatives

It is possible to control and organize teaching by sheer force of personality. However, the most likely alternative to classroom routine is chaos. At the very least you will waste time and energy trying to get things done. Most of us prefer the security of routines.

Avoid

Arbitrary change.

Any suggestion that the routine is unimportant.

12 SEATING PLANS

My pupils want to sit with friends but I think they'll distract each other.

Description

When pupils enter your classroom for the first time you can either give them the choice of where to sit or decide for them. Your choice may depend on seating by ability, alternating seating by gender, separating known trouble-makers or allowing friendship groups.

Giving pupils the choice potentially puts power in their hands; being decisive about where they sit demonstrates that it is your classroom and you are in charge.

Cause

Giving them the choice first then imposing changes is the worst option as they will have settled and will feel aggrieved that you are invading their space. Pupils create their own space in classrooms and generally feel unhappy about changing partners, friends and room positions.

Action

Create a seating plan before your first lesson and enforce it in the face of grumbles. Even an alphabetical plan has at least the advantage of helping you learn their names. However, some research about pupils' ability, friendship groups – or, more importantly, an awareness of people who should *not* sit next to each other – will stand you in good stead. Ask previous teachers, form tutors and year heads if they have any views based on their experience. If possible ask pupils themselves for their preferences in a confidential questionnaire.

Make it clear from the start that you reserve the right to move anyone at any time for any reason, and implement this to split up conflicts and behaviour which hinders learning.

Priorities

Demonstrating who is in control.

Creating an effective learning environment.

Alternatives

If you have your own classroom you have the great benefit of being able to arrange tables as you wish. Consider the advantages of rows, columns, clusters; directional facing to the whiteboard, computers, display boards, etc.

If you use other people's rooms you may struggle to use other people's layouts and find it a bad start to the lesson if you have to move chairs and tables. Nevertheless it is worth persisting on occasions at least to make the most of a discussion in a circle and group work in clusters as well as more formal didactic learning in rows. If you have two or three preferred layouts use them frequently, then pupils will become used to them and disruption will be less.

First Aid Kit for Teachers

Avoid

Giving free choice then taking it away.

Pupils telling you they won't move 'because you said we could sit here.'

13 COPING WITH YOUR OWN ANGER OR STRONG EMOTION

I'm bursting with frustration and anger with a class!

Description

Pupils can be frustrating and infuriating. It would be impossible, maybe even unwise, not to show anger at times. However you should aim to control your anger and target it. The same goes for coping with angry pupils and parents. It is natural to feel anger, but it's what you do with it that counts.

Cause

Repeated illogical, rude, offensive, behaviour by pupils.

Offensive, aggressive parents.

Stress on you from overwork, personal problems, pressure from all sides.

Ideally, you should separate the unacceptable pupil behaviour from the stress caused by other factors. However, being under stress, you can't, which makes it worse.

Action

If it is one or two pupils who are causing the immediate problem, move them to another part of the room or out of the room entirely. Tell them clearly – and if necessary more than once – that they must move/leave the room.

In the event of a refusal, use the following: 'I have been reasonable. I have asked you several times to leave the room. Are you refusing to follow my reasonable instruction? Then I'll get someone else to deal with you.'

Call for assistance and as calmly as possible explain that you will not have this pupil in your classroom.

It does not help to be emotional at this stage. Emphasize the way they are preventing others from learning/refusing to obey your reasonable instructions. If you need to leave the room briefly to call for assistance, do your best to ensure the class is safe. Giving a minute for the child to reconsider their situation without you there can be helpful.

Priorities

Looking after yourself.

Amending the behaviour or stopping the situation while remaining professionally detached if at all possible.

Moving pupil(s) away to separate them from the cause of their anger and an audience for their behaviour and your reaction.

If you can control your anger and bottle it up for a short time, do so. Better to burst into tears in the staffroom than in the classroom.

Alternatives

Show resigned determination. Hold down the anger. Breathe deeply and let it out in a long sigh. Deepen your voice and try to control any wavering in it. A roar is more effective than a scream. Speak with deliberation and emphasis. Show you mean business.

Walk away from the cause of your anger, but only when someone else can take control. There is no shame in this. A different face will usually have the advantage and can seize the initiative.

Consider walking away permanently. This is a serious step but not an inconceivable one. There may come a time when it's all too much. If the pupils appal you, the job seems simply not worth it and you are unable to teach the way you want to, going might be better all round. Walking away from the classroom is better than hitting someone, saying something you may regret or damaging yourself. However, do not take this step without giving due time for calm consideration. Don't let the buggers grind you down.

Avoid

Swearing. Even if pupils do.

Stopping a really angry pupil from leaving the room.

Any physical confrontation. I know of a teacher who, confronted in class by a violent parent, kept his hands stiffly by his sides to avoid any suggestion of retaliation. Superhuman perhaps, but a case of superb professional valour deserving a medal.

Screaming and shrieking (unless actually injured).

Threatening anything you can't carry out.

14 COPING WITH A PUPIL'S ANGER

What do I do when a pupil is taking out his frustrations on me? I haven't done anything wrong!

Description

Pupils can be frustrating and infuriating. They can also be frustrated and infuriated. They may have to cope with problems at home or with erratic friends while coping with the changes caused by their own adolescence.

Ideally we should aim to help them control their own anger. But we may also have another 30 pupils to look after and keep safe. Every situation is different, but we might distinguish between angry shouting on the one hand and physically dangerous behaviour on the other, which requires different strategies.

Cause

Adolescents undergo significant changes in their hormones which affect their bodies and their brains, and thence their emotions and their behaviour. Young children may simply have no sense of self-control.

Any child can have experiences at home which adversely affect their ability to deal with the routines of school. The teacher is a focus for their attention and can be the focus for their fury. In an odd way the fact that they view you as a focus for their anger means that you really are the authority figure you've been trying to be!

Action

Show by your words, your tone of voice and your body language that you want them to calm down. Minor demonstrations of anger can be dealt with by ignoring the pupil and encouraging the rest of the class to carry on as normal. Significant anger, however, has to be literally faced up to. Eye contact with a suitable facial expression, open hands and calming gestures can help even when the child's fury means he/she can't hear your words.

Persist in being reasonable in the face of their unreasonableness.

Suggest alternatives: that they sit down; that they cool off outside. Open the door and stand nearby but without blocking it. Provide a clear exit route if they are clearly bigger and angrier than you.

Priorities

Safety. If the child is attacking you or other pupils this must be stopped. Sometimes other children pile in to 'help' which, while commendable, is tricky and can get out of hand. Nevertheless you'll appreciate it if the child is attacking you .... . Preventing self-harm is very tricky. Unless you know the child has a history of injuring him/herself it may be best to let the child's fury burn out.

Summon assistance. Use a panic button or a phone. Send a child to get help from the nearest classroom or office. Do nothing to further antagonize the angry child – now is not the time for reckless bravery, it's the time for calm, being firm but cautious.

Establish the level of threat. If the child is wielding a weapon or is big and strong enough to injure you, is he/she likely to injure pupils or just you?

Stand within reach of the door. If the child is not using it as an escape route, it may be your best option.

Alternatives

If he/she refuses to leave the room, consider letting all the other pupils leave, in single file.

Angry young children can be calmed by wrapping them firmly in your arms until their fury is past. This is not generally a good idea for adolescent pupils. However, if you can restrain them by firmly holding their wrists to their sides, it could help. It is recommended that you also repeat something like, 'I am not going to harm you. Stop struggling and I will let go.'

Avoid

Shutting the door or blocking an escape route.

Reacting with violence or anger.

Initiating physical contact (apart from restraint techniques, as above).

At all costs avoid hitting the pupil. An arm hold or pushing away may be accepted if you are avoiding injury, but anything interpreted as attack is never acceptable.

Endangering other pupils.

15 GETTING ATTENTION

How do I get them to listen to me?

Description

You rightly demand and require attention. Without it there can be little successful learning and no respect from pupils. However, simply walking into a room and shouting 'Be quiet!' doesn't always work.

Cause

In many schools it is no longer an automatic response to be quiet when the teacher comes into the room. The days when pupils stood up as the teacher entered the room are over. Respect now has to be earned. Obedience is not automatic.

Action

1. Use what residual respect there may be for an adult and build on it.
2. Stand firmly, chin up and with as much confidence as you can muster in a visible position.
3. Clap your hands once or twice and engage eye contact.
4. In a level voice loud enough to reach the back of the room say that you expect silence before you convey your message.
5. Nod approvingly at those who stop talking; stare out any who continue to talk.
6. Have something genuine and useful to say.
7. Wait. Repeat if necessary.
8. Thank those who were quiet.
9. If this is a class you will be meeting frequently, explain to them the need for attention. Do this at the beginning, before they have a chance to subvert you. Impose it regularly so their reaction becomes automatic.

Priorities

Absolute silence. No half measures.
Look serious; adopt 'the teacher's stare'.
Have something worth saying, say it concisely, then move on.

Alternatives

1. With a biddable class, instead of a clap, click your fingers at two-second intervals. With luck a ripple of silence will flow from front to back of the classroom. Expect silence before you reach the fifth click and praise the class if they achieve silence before the fifth click.
2. Draw a circle on the board. Add straight lines from 12 o'clock clockwise until the class is quiet. Explain that this is a clock recording how long they will stay behind after class if they continue to fail to listen to you. Say: 'You waste my time and I'll waste yours.' However, note that

keeping back the whole class when another class is due in the room, or when there are buses waiting to take the pupils home, will cause serious problems.

3.   Have the class leave the room if they are already there and line up in silence in the corridor. Tell them that the noise is unacceptable. Have them file in past you in silence.

4.   During a lesson when you want silent work, say you *will* have silence for five minutes. Explain that anyone who breaks the silence will extend that time by a further five minutes. Count down 5, 4, 3, 2, 1 and if there is not silence add the extra five minutes immediately.

5.   Combine the clock and the five-minute-silence strategies.

Avoid

Backing down on the need for silent attention.

Raise your voice but do not scream (teachers with high-pitched voices beware!).

Never threaten anything you cannot carry out (but have faith you'll achieve silence).

16 PROSECUTION FOR YOUR ACTIONS

What if I end up in court?

Description

Most of us naturally avoid confrontation. You may cross the road to avoid a violent drunkard and you will think twice before wading in to someone else's domestic incident.

However teachers have a duty of care, a professional duty to maintain discipline and a personal duty to maintain standards and respect. If you walk away from incidents you may be neglecting your duty. You are unlikely to gain respect by being seen to avoid a problem.

If you act unprofessionally with children – or parents – by inappropriate restraint or language, or by improperly confiscating personal equipment, you are open to at least criticism and at most prosecution. We need to know where the boundaries lie, yet they are changing and are unclear.

The DfES boundaries (circular 10/98) are that the teacher is authorized:

> to use such force as is reasonable in all the circumstances to prevent a pupil from doing, or continuing to do, any of the following:

- committing a criminal offence . . .;
- injuring themselves or others;
- causing damage to property . . .;
- engaging in any behaviour prejudicial to maintaining good order and discipline at the school or among any of its pupils.... . (Section 550A)

The Act allows all teachers at a school to use *reasonable and proportionate force* to control or restrain pupils.

Cause

One obvious cause is society's change in respect for authority. Some blame this on social revolution, some on the turmoil of two world wars. Some see it as a positive effect of having young people question the *status quo* and think for themselves. Whatever the reason it is a fact that teachers wield less power and influence over their pupils than they did a generation ago.

Physical contact and the cane are forbidden. Detention and confiscation are now less likely to be supported by parents, who are more likely to side with their children than with the school.

Moves by government to give teachers immunity from prosecution in some disciplinary situations have fallen foul of human rights legislation. As things stand the false accuser may have a right of anonymity while the falsely accused teacher is publicly named. Even if found innocent, mud sticks.

Action

The key issue is establishing good order.

To establish this, try reasoning. If that is impossible, try offering alternatives. 'Either you put that away now or will be forced to confiscate it. It's your decision.'

Where possible, continue reasoning and give a clear and final warning before acting – if action is necessary. This supports any future action you may take and a clear final warning could avoid any action at all.

There is no obligation on you to intervene if there is a real danger that you will be injured. In this case you must send for help and continue trying to reason and calm down the pupil.

Act with conspicuous restraint. Never attack. Avoid losing your temper. You are permitted to defend yourself and others but do not allow defence to become attack. Stand your ground but do not move forward. Block their path in one direction by standing in a position where their escape in another direction is their easiest option.

Usher without physical contact if possible. If necessary lead them by the hand or arm or place a hand in the centre of their back, but consider that even mild physical contact can produce a disproportionately angry reaction. Attempts by government to allow teachers to use 'reasonable force' to escort an uncooperative pupil from class may 'breach the right to respect for private life and to dignity and physical integrity' of the child. Which is nonsense.

By the way, now is not the time to argue that the child's actions may breach your respect and dignity. Save that for later. This is first aid.

The government does believe 'that teachers must have a clear right to discipline unruly pupils, otherwise the rights of other pupils to an orderly education are threatened' (*Daily Mail*, 15 May 2006). However, as yet there is no clear definition of how to do this. Circular 10/98, section 6 notes:

> There is no legal definition of 'reasonable force'. So it is not possible to set out comprehensively when it is reasonable to use force, or the degree of force that may reasonably be used. It will always depend on all the circumstances of the case.

So tread warily.

Priorities

Establishing good order.
  Action without force or any form of bullying.

Alternatives

Walk briskly towards the scene, calling out loudly. With luck, warning of your approach can mean physical intervention is avoided.

Avoid

Unreasonable force.
  Believing your innocence is self-evident.
  Being heroic.

PART 2 ACADEMIC

The academic side of teaching is more than simply conveying a body of knowledge. Dickens' Gradgrind may see his pupils as 'little pitchers ... who were to be filled so full of facts' but we know that on a day-to-day basis the curriculum is sometimes lost in the pressure of pupils who can't or won't learn and in our continued efforts to develop effective teaching strategies.

1 RUNNING OUT OF MATERIAL

I find myself worrying about not having enough to occupy the class for an hour!

Description
New teachers are often worried about this. I have seen student teachers just clam up because they've run out of things to say. Experienced teachers never run out of things to say (though sometimes you may wish they would ...).

Cause
Lack of preparation or faulty timing are likely causes. Experience gives you a good idea of how long things last, and you learn that activities often take longer than you expect when you include tidying away and giving out homework.

Another cause is telling the class too much and not giving them time either to absorb the information, ask questions or do something with what you've told them. You don't have to talk all the time and you don't have to be the centre of attention. Give them an activity to help them absorb what you've told them.

Action
Remember that pupils are supposed to work too. You talk less so they may work more. In case there is time in hand, have ready some of the following:

- Prepare some standard drills or games to test learning or skills. Try quick-fire questions, a spelling test, quiz on safety rules, sentences featuring grammatical errors or maths speed tests. Have one half of the class suggest answers to which the other half have to find questions.
- Have the pupils each find five recently learned facts about your topic and test each other in pairs – then swap pairs.
- Spend more time than usual carefully setting homework and ask the pupils about likely issues.
- Have pupils 'mark' each other's written work. Have them do this in pencil.

Encourage them to be critical of each other's work by giving positive advice and helpful suggestions. Explain you will be checking their comments too.

- Ask for ideas on how pupils would solve the world's problems and choose problems which match your current topic. Look for creative answers.
- Start a general discussion about what pupils like or don't like about this subject or this topic.
- Discuss learning targets and what pupils could do to improve.
- Explain how this lesson fits into the other lessons on this topic and what you hope to do in the next lesson. You do know, don't you?

Priorities

Stay in charge. Don't just let the class drift into nattering among themselves but define time slots. Tell pupils they have five minutes to discuss the current topic and be prepared to come up with a point of view or a question. Then you ask for a couple of sample responses. Show them the task was important.

Alternatives

If you can see this problem recurring, consider encouraging pupils to bring in relevant resources and asking them to talk about what they've brought. A collection of clippings and objects is a great source of inspiration. However, don't invite them to bring things in without making use of them.

Avoid

Standing like a dummy and looking lost.

2. TIMING OF LESSONS

The end of the lesson is chaos when I overrun a good lesson!

Description

Preparation of activities involves allocating time and checking that the timing is right. However long the activity is, if you have lunch or the end of school or if another class is baying outside, you simply can't overrun.

Cause

Assuming you know the lesson times, causes of overrunning may be poor planning or failure to check on progress (more likely if you're enjoying it, but that's no excuse). However a watch and a classroom clock which don't agree can cause chaos.

The problem then becomes, how do you dismiss the class in an orderly fashion (which is important) while clearing the room and its equipment.

Action

Always use a reliable watch and check it against school time.

Do look at timing and calculate the time remaining.

Give advance warnings: only ten minutes left . . . you have five minutes, start packing up now . . . two minutes – stop now!

Messy activities obviously need more tidying time so aim to finish well in advance. Even if everyone is standing by their tables with several minutes to go you can always find some scraps of paper on the floor, a book out of place and still have time to summarize the activity, what they've learned and how it leads in to the next lesson.

If that bell has gone and it's too late to avoid it, let them out rapidly but not in a disorderly way – row by row or table by table – while making a quick check on litter. This can be fast but appears organized. Apologize to the incoming teacher or class and resolve not to do it again.

Priorities

Keep to time.

Alternatives

Use a travel clock on your desk. But avoid loud alarms.

Demand a good clock in your room, in a position so you can see it rather than the pupils.

Use a noiseless alert on your electronic whiteboard or your mobile phone.

In extremis ask a pupil to give you a time check five minutes before the end of the lesson – but ask individually, or the whole class will 'help' by clock watching.

Avoid

Overrunning.

Believing your pearls of wisdom are important enough to delay the timetable.

Letting pupils leave in a mob – especially while cuttings and detritus cover the floor.

3 EXAMINATIONS

I want to treat exams seriously but pupils overreact.

Description

Exams are formal events intended to test learning under strictly enforced conditions. Whether you agree with them or not is not a point of discussion at exam time. It is your role to uphold them and to approach them in a serious way. This is as true for SATS as it is for A levels.

Cause

Problems can be caused beforehand by poor teacher planning and during exam time by not following the strict examination rules.

Pupil indiscipline has the potential for causing disruption but is less likely if the absolute seriousness of exams is emphasized from the beginning. A wry acceptance of the inevitability of examinations is fine, but making fun of them is not.

I used to tell of the (possibly apocryphal) case of two examination candidates, seated at either side of the exam room, who were found to have colluded. I explained that, not only were the two guilty parties subsequently banned from all examinations but all the other candidates sitting between them also had their papers cancelled. This seemed to help my pupils treat exams seriously. It's an effective scare story, true or not.

Action
Teachers

Plan for the correct syllabus, identifying likely questions, optimum method and give practice in examination conditions. Follow up practice essays with a detailed analysis of the way the questions were answered and suggestions for better answers. Help candidates understand how the elements of the course fit together so they have a holistic view as well as a detailed understanding.

Invigilators

Impose examination conditions including rituals of arriving in good time, switching off mobile phones, leaving bags and coats in a separate area, being silent from the moment of entering the examination room, being seated in an orderly fashion according to a prearranged pattern.

Patrol the room with a serious and alert face.

Have one invigilator at the back of the hall as well as one at the front.

Keep as alert as possible – any delay in answering a candidate's request for extra paper is a measure of your inattention.

Treat all subjects and all examinations equally seriously.

Ensure you can contact the examinations officer.

Record the time and candidate numbers of any incidents. Mark and sign a candidate's paper at the point they had reached at the time of the incident.

The School

In assemblies and your own lessons alert the whole school to the importance of being quiet around exam rooms. This builds up a necessary respect for exams throughout the whole school.

Be clear about your procedures for candidates who don't turn up on time, who leave the room early, who are suspected of cheating or are sick during the examination. Do you phone home? How long do you wait before they are refused entry?

Be clear about procedures for fire alarms during an examination. The school may decide candidates should ignore a fire alarm unless there is a specific warning from a senior teacher. Be prepared to reassure candidates that this will have no adverse effect on marking.

Priorities

Follow both the letter and the spirit of the regulations as given by the examination board.

Make sure you know which exams allow equipment and which do not.

Make sure you know what to do when a pupil wants to leave the room, when one disrupts proceedings or when one arrives late.

Record any transgressions and report to your school examinations officer.

Alternatives

There are no alternatives to the seriousness with which examinations must be taken.

There are, however, stages of seriousness leading up to examinations. Revision, planning and practice can be done in an entertaining way, made into a competition or a game, regarded with a shrug of inevitability – but never mocked.

Avoid

Misinterpretation of syllabus.

Teaching the wrong syllabus.

Treating examinations lightly.

4 COURSEWORK

Coursework is great teaching but it's been heavily criticized as an assessment tool. How do I deal with it?

Description

Coursework has had a bad press in recent years. Whereas at first it was seen to be a sensible alternative to the 'sudden death' of examinations, it has more recently been open to allegations of interference by parents and by teachers.

The maximum percentage which coursework can contribute to a whole syllabus has been gradually reduced.

Coursework is as much a process as an outcome. As a process it has considerable benefits to the pupil, teaching skills of writing, preparation, study and information literacy, and personal responsibility. As an outcome it is difficult to compare it to an examination script, because it is assessing an entirely different thing. However, if its outcome is not to be formally assessed, the process will be weakened. Pupils will not take it so seriously if it does not count towards their final grade.

Cause

The causes of public doubt of coursework can be summed up as plagiarism, interference and lack of rigour. The long road of coursework does not compare favourably with the short burst of a three-hour examination. This is both unfair and counter-educational. However it is true that it is difficult to detect the subtler kind of input by parents and difficult to draw a line between fair suggestions and unfair contributions by a teacher.

Action

- Understand from the beginning the difference between accepted assistance and unfair practices. The former is a necessary part of teaching; the latter is doing too much of the work for the pupil. All parties must understand this. The Examination Board will have clear advice, which should be followed by teachers, pupils and parents.
- At the same time take the opportunity to explain the good side of coursework – the opportunity to follow your own interests, to plan and research independently, to work practically in real conditions, and to produce something you can be proud of and which can be a point of discussion at interviews.
- Ensure the task is appropriate and as original as possible. Avoid titles which you know have been widely studied before. Add conditions to popular titles such as '... with particular reference to ...' or '... in nineteenth-century Yorkshire ...'.
- Follow the drafts of the coursework at every stage, and keep the drafts as proof of progress. Insist that references are properly acknowledged. Have pupils sign an agreement to follow the Examination Board rules – and have this countersigned by parents or guardians.

- Explain the importance of the structure of the work, planning headings and subheadings at an early stage, following the sections as advised by the Board.
- Follow the criteria of the Board for marking. Explain these criteria to pupils and show what must be present for a good grade.
- Follow up any signs of plagiarism. Require the pupil to give the source of the material. Type a few suspect phrases into a good search engine to see if they match online sources.
- Be very firm about deadlines, allowing good time for internal marking if necessary.

Priorities
Stay legal. Help and guide without contributing significantly to the finished piece.

Alternatives
The obvious alternative to coursework is 100 per cent examination. A less obvious alternative is for coursework to be carried out in supervised conditions. This could be too time-consuming to be practical in the classroom, but there are intermediate stages where perhaps materials are brought in to the classroom but all written work is completed under the supervision of a teacher or invigilator – and not necessarily in strict silence or normal examination conditions.

Avoid
Unchecked copying.

Favouritism – either towards pupil or subject matter.

Comparing coursework with examinations. They should complement each other.

5 HOMEWORK

Homework is a real pain! More marking for me and more aggro when they don't do it!

Description

Homework is contentious. Often it is perceived as gratuitous extra work and a penance for everyone – teacher, pupil and parent. Checking up on it often causes aggravation which then begins the next lesson negatively.

While we can't avoid it being a burden without cancelling it altogether, we can try to minimize the damage, rationalize its purpose and show how it can be useful.

Cause

It seems to be extra work, so try to integrate it into the lesson.

Compare: '... and class, just do the next exercise for homework and bring it in tomorrow. OK, you can go ...', with: 'We've looked at the first part in class, so I want you to look on the way home for examples of what we've been talking about. Write them down so we can all share them next lesson. Now we'll start looking at the second part ...'.

The former seems – and is – rushed, an afterthought, an extra, a burden. The second is part of the lesson, builds on class work and is a practical activity which couldn't be done in the classroom. It supplements and complements.

Action

Set a coursework task which involves time spent at home or in the library doing research. You can allocate homework time to extend limited lesson time, setting a written task which might take five hours of which three are in class and two are at home. If the pupil doesn't use the allocated time, that's their own responsibility and they will face the consequences.

Homework is ideal for asking questions, collecting items to show in class, contacting the community, revising and redrafting, doing surveys of your street or television adverts or collecting observations of the environment. Homework is ideal for interviewing relatives, neighbours and shopkeepers or collecting family photographs for an autobiography project. However, for any of this do give adequate time.

Priorities

Make homework part of a lesson, plan it as carefully as the rest of the lesson, set it early, define it clearly, make it relevant – to this and the next lesson, know what the school expects in terms of quality, frequency and length. Use it, collect it or mark it. Treat it as a valuable thing and make it worthwhile for the pupil to complete it. Record whether homework has been done successfully and praise pupils for prompt and accurate homework in their reports.

Alternatives

Integration with class work.

Setting activities which clearly cannot be done in the classroom (collecting, interviewing, researching, etc.).

To make it a policy that homework is never set is probably unwise as it weakens the necessary link between school work and daily life.

Avoid

Treating homework as an afterthought.

Treating it as superfluous.

Setting any significant homework to be handed in the next day. Pupils have a right to organize their lives too.

6 ASKING THE RIGHT QUESTIONS

When I ask the class a question they either don't answer or they all shout out at once!

Description

Listen to an experienced teacher asking questions and getting answers. There are closed questions and open questions and each one is used deliberately to open up a discussion or to eliminate the possibility of an inappropriate response.

Compare: 'Have you all got books?' with: 'Is there anyone who has *not* got a book?'

The former apparently requires an answer from all pupils who do have books while the latter requires a response only from the one or two who do not. The former stimulates a hubbub while the second, especially with the emphasis on *not*, should generate silence from the majority.

Cause

A lively class can take advantage of a rhetorical question and pretend an answer is needed. They will take every opportunity to call out or interrupt.

You need to show them when you want answers and when you want silent attention.

A further cause may be that you've not made it clear how you want the pupils to answer. Do you insist on hands up and you choose or do you appreciate spontaneous calls? Do you get annoyed when several call out but are grateful when just one calls out? What do you think pupils make of that? Might they just find it easier not to try?

Action

Think about whether you want clear-cut answers or whether you are encouraging open discussion. Choose your questions to elicit these responses.

Say 'Is there anyone who does *not* understand?' not 'Does everyone understand?'

In the corridor ask 'Where *should* you be?' not 'What do you think you're doing?' The answer to the latter will probably be 'Nothing', which gets you nowhere. The answer to the former will be 'Room 123' so you can say, 'Well, get there now!'

Priorities

Remain in charge.

Be able to keep order at all times.

Direct questioning where you, the educator, know is most useful.

Alternatives

Leave questions to the pupils. Brainstorming questions which are then written down and considered methodically can provide the mixture of spontaneous enthusiasm and calm answers you are looking for.

Questions sealed in envelopes and placed in boxes are another approach. Just

be prepared to ignore the questions which are placed there to antagonize you
. . . .

Avoid

Asking rhetorical questions.

Asking questions which are essentially 'Guess what's in my head?' It may be logical to you to ask that question, but it's because you already know the answer. Your pupils are not so fortunate!

7 GENERAL REFUSAL TO WORK

I teach children who just refuse to work!

Description

Doing mundane school work doesn't suit everyone. Methods of working have to be demonstrated and learned. Pupils need to be shown how to write an essay, how to learn vocabulary, how to organize and present things.

Cause

Some pupils simply find things too difficult and resolve the issue by refusal. Some refuse because it is expected by their peer group.

Some refuse because they don't like you or find the subject 'boring'.

Some pupils are simply lazy or have other things on their minds.

It may or may not be a good enough excuse, but it can help to find out the reasons for refusal.

Action

Talk to other teachers and to parents. Find out any obvious reasons for refusal. Consider home problems, friendship problems, specific learning difficulties, eyesight, etc.

Although there should be no need to pander to the tastes of idle and demanding pupils (or their parents), remember that good teaching and interesting lessons help to reduce the amount of bad behaviour.

If possible coax rather than complain. Well, it's worth it if it works . . . .

Record examples of incomplete and inadequate work. You might identify a pattern, and you will be able to report accurately.

Remember also that, even if a lesson *is* boring, that is absolutely no excuse for failing to do the work set.

Priorities

Identify the problem.

Solve the problem before it spreads and infects the whole class. Tackle it actively; it's unlikely to go away.

Aim to make your lessons appropriate, with varied learning methods and differentiation. At least you'll be able to rebut the claim that your classes are boring.

Keep the pupil up to date with work. Falling behind in understanding simply compounds the problem.

Alternatives

Detentions during which outstanding work is completed.

Moving the pupil to another class (not generally advised).

Avoid

Ignoring the issue.

Lengthy unbroken periods of writing.

8 COVER LESSONS – TAKING

I have to cover someone else's class while they're away!

Description

You are told you must take someone else's class when you would otherwise have a non-contact lesson. There may or may not be work set, but the chances are that you would rather be doing something else.

Cause

Someone has to cover lessons for absent colleagues. Mostly this is an imposition on you who already have more than enough to do. It causes you stress. However, the school budget may dictate that paying a specialist cover teacher for short term absences is impossible.

In a small primary school the Head may use his/her non-teaching time to take the class, but this adds to his/her burden. The class may be amalgamated with other classes, but this makes it more difficult for the teachers of these classes – and their pupils.

If the absence is caused by illness, this may in itself be a result of a stressful workplace.

Action

Think positive and be prepared. Though your heart may sink, treat it as an opportunity to see children you know in a different situation and make an impression on children who don't know you.

Always have at least one idea up your sleeve to occupy a class for an hour. Something which allows you ten minutes to interact with the class followed by a long period of quiet pupil work is ideal. 'Continue with what you were doing last lesson' may be unsatisfactory for you if you don't know exactly what is expected and pupils could take advantage of this.

Do be firm and take control, even if your instinct and your need is to hide away in marking or admin. This is an excellent opportunity for you to make an impression on other pupils, whom you may have to teach later.

Priorities

Care for the pupils.
  Keep calm.

Alternatives

Clarify your school's procedures for setting work for absent colleagues. Whose responsibility is it?

Clarify your school's policy on non-contact time. You should have a set minimum of non-contact time. The Head can also request you to undertake reasonable extra duties – but how are cover lessons shared out? Are they allocated fairly? Understanding and having faith in a fair system goes a long way to putting up with the inevitable burden.

Avoid

Taking your stress out on the children. It's not their fault – they'd probably rather have their usual class teacher too.

Taking your stress out on the person who has to organize the cover.

9 COVER LESSONS – GIVING

I have to leave work for a class while I'm away!

Description

Planning an interesting lesson for someone else to teach is not easy. But it must be planned and it must be fail-safe.

Cause

If this is a planned absence for a meeting or a course, you should build it into your lesson scheme as soon as you know of it. However, when you're too ill to go to school you may be unable to plan work for your class. Yet someone has to do it and usually you're the one.

If you have a coordinator or a head of department to cover for you, you should at least make sure they know what you are currently teaching so the work can fit in with your previous lessons.

Action

If it's a planned absence, be punctilious about setting up the work, providing a formal lesson plan, including what the cover teacher should do and say, where the resources are, where the pupils' books are, details of seating arrangements and what is the expected outcome by the end of the lesson. Keep this detailed information clear and simple so the cover teacher can grab the plan and carry it out faultlessly.

Agree a standard format for your school cover lessons – an A4 sheet with spaces for teacher name, class name, subject, date and lesson, room, class list, resources, instructions. Standardizing should make it easier for any teacher to set work and any cover teacher to follow.

Priorities

Make work available which will be educational, will occupy the pupils and is easy for a non-specialist to supervise.

Alternatives

In departments compile a batch of 'instant' lessons for all occasions, subject-focused but accessible at all levels of ability and age. These are to be used in emergencies, not as replacements for thoughtful, planned cover work.

Avoid

Leaving the problem to the cover teacher.

Making the work too elaborate for the cover teacher to follow.

Work which requires specialist knowledge

Work which can be misinterpreted or wilfully misunderstood by the pupils.

10 SUPPLY TEACHERS

I'm on supply – what should I do?

Description

Supply teachers make a full-time job out of doing what full-time teachers often see as a burden. But it need not be a burden, and it's only as full-time as the need and the choice allow. While some supply teachers see it as a bridge between other jobs, some choose to do so because of the variety it offers. I know one supply teacher who was so good at his job that he was offered a permanent post – and promptly resigned.

Cause

While cover teachers normally look after classes for immediate sickness or emergency, the supply teacher is employed to cover planned absence or long-term sickness. Or that's the theory. In practice the supply teacher may be contacted only hours before arriving at the school. So the first motto is 'Be prepared.'

Action

Decide on your personal priorities. Are you doing this long or short term? Is it for the money, the experience, as a bridge between jobs or the freedom to choose where and what you will do today without the need for lesson preparation, marking or report writing. Are you willing to work at any school or only a limited few?

Use these decisions to make your mind up whether today you stay in bed, spend a day in the garden or take maths with Year 9 on the other side of town.

Register with the local authority to get on their supply list.

Make sure you are CRB-checked – and carry a copy of that certificate as proof.

Contact schools you would be happy to work at and make yourself known to them.

Prepare several 'lessons for all occasions' so if you do get landed without instructions or materials you can still cope.

Don't be too choosy when you start as a supply teacher. Use the experience of different schools, subjects and systems to inform your knowledge of education. You can become more selective later if you wish.

Priorities

Use this as a learning experience.

Be willing, confident, competent, prompt and capable. You can and should be all these things because you have the priceless knowledge that you don't absolutely need to be there tomorrow. And you have no marking tonight.

Ensure you have clear instructions, a map of the site, a bag of emergency lessons and you are familiar with the basic school rules.

Announce your name to each class and write it clearly. Be firm from the beginning. If absolutely necessary be prepared to override the set lesson in order to impose order and control.

Alternatives

Use this variety of experience to write a sitcom, novel or exposé of modern education/youth culture/yob rule.

Decide on the system/school/age group/subject specialism you prefer and consider applying full time. If you're any good, the school you've provided supply teaching for will snap you up.

Avoid

Criticizing one school to another.

Criticizing the absent teacher.

Walking out in the middle of the day protesting that the kids are awful.

PART 3 SPECIAL NEEDS AND MEDICAL

Every child has special needs – and so have teachers. It's just that some children have more specialized and specific needs than others. Non-expert teachers should not diagnose but should observe children and alert specialists to possible problems.

1 EPILEPSY

A child in my class has epilepsy – what should I look for?

Description

Epilepsy is a tendency to have seizures. They usually only last for seconds or a few minutes. Teachers are in a good position to identify symptoms. They may need to deal with a seizure and follow up by giving reassurance to the patient and the rest of the class afterwards.

A detailed individual health-care plan for every pupil with the condition can be a way of alerting teachers to a problem and this plan should be available to all teachers.

Symptoms may include twitching, an unusual taste in the mouth, confusion and a tendency to wander. The most serious type of seizure is the grand mal where the child will lose consciousness, have convulsions and breathing may become difficult for a few minutes.

Cause

Seizures are caused by electrical activity in the brain and can affect people at any time.

Action

In the event of a child having a seizure:

- Stay calm, and reassure others in the class.
- Make sure that the child cannot harm themself.
- Only move the child if there is a possibility of them hurting themself.
- Cushion the child's head with something soft.
- Do not restrict the child's movements.
- Do not put anything in the child's mouth, including food or drink.
- Loosen any tight clothing around the neck.

- Once a convulsive seizure has stopped, place the child in the recovery position and remain with the child until they are fully recovered.
- Reassure the child and allow them to rest and/or sleep, as necessary, in a supervised, quiet place such as a medical room.

Note that the Epilepsy Foundation says:

> Perhaps the most persistent myth is that a person having a seizure can swallow his tongue. It is not physically possible to swallow your tongue. The tongue, if relaxed, could possibly block the breathing passage. The way to avoid this is to turn the person on their side so the tongue falls away to the side of the mouth. ('Communicating about epilepsy')

In PE, climbing and swimming, practical science or technology lessons extra supervision will be required.

Priorities

Stay calm.

Reassure everyone.

Prevent injury while a convulsion is taking place.

If the seizure lasts for more than five minutes, or if there are breathing difficulties, call an ambulance.

Alternatives

Confusion, a dreamy state, twitching or wandering, which the child has no memory of later, could be signs of epilepsy. Check with parents immediately.

The child could be allowed to sleep at the back of the class or taken elsewhere to rest.

If medication is necessary, be very wary of volunteering to administer it. Some treatments require rectal insertion.

Avoid

Alarming the child or the rest of the class.

Injury.

In a potentially epileptic child try to avoid anxiety and stress, flashing lights, stark geometric patterns.

2 DYSLEXIA

A child in my class is struggling with spelling, writing or reading, yet in many ways seems quite able. Could he be dyslexic, and how can I find out?

Description

Dyslexia comes from the Greek meaning 'difficulty with words'. Many dyslexics describe the page as having letters bouncing around on it, making reading difficult.

Once described as a middle-class problem because concerned parents attributed slow progress in their children to dyslexia rather than accept they were not able readers, dyslexia is undoubtedly a real problem which should be tackled as soon as it is identified.

The British Dyslexia Association publishes a valuable range of features to look for and suggestions for coping with dyslexia. Look for a significant contrast between good oral skills and weak or slow word-processing skills. Written work is likely to be untidy, perhaps phonetic, with crossing out of words spelled in several ways, perhaps with letters in the wrong order, upper-case and lower-case letters mixed up, or similar-looking letters often confused.

Reading is slow, comprehension is limited, with words omitted and the pupil having difficulty in recognizing the beginnings and endings of words.

Behaviour may be 'dreamy' with lack of concentration, or disruptive in frustration. The child may be forgetful and disorganized with equipment and arrangements.

There may also be numeracy problems, confusion with directions, difficulty retaining several instructions at once.

Cause

Dyslexia adversely affects learning in one or more of reading, spelling and writing. Weaknesses may be in speed of processing, short-term memory, organization, sequencing and spoken language and motor skills. Part of the problem may be eye weaknesses.

Action

Talk to your Special Educational Needs Coordinator (SENCO).

Carry out an assessment at school (easiest if you have a suitably qualified teacher on the staff but tests are widely available) and consider referral to an educational psychologist which may lead to an individual learning plan. Also recommend an eye test.

With younger children in particular, encourage the child to write using the 'continuous cursive' style rather than printing separate letters. Offer wide-lined paper, a good HB pencil (not a ballpoint) or special grip on a handwriting pen. Supervise good posture and a book which slants to the left for the right-hander.

Encourage typing skills at an early stage.

Ensure special arrangements have been made for SATS and other examinations. For SATS, notify your local authority. GCSE examinations will require an educational psychologist's report, which may take considerable time to obtain.

Priorities

Early assessment. If a problem is identified, your recommendation that a child be assessed will set the wheels in motion to help the child.

Be realistic about the length of time it may take for an educational psychologist to be available.

Use appropriate activities with the child to enable them to take part in classroom learning.

Alternatives

Many dyslexics find a word processor frees their creativity, enabling drafting and a neat final product. Encourage children to word-process their work and show them how to use the grammar and dictionary tools to improve their work.

Demonstrate speaking-text, speech-recognition software.

Encourage practice using typing programs.

Use colour-tinted gels overlaid on a printed page. This has been shown to help some readers.

Avoid

Confusing low skills or intelligence with dyslexia.

Being patronizing to parents who claim their child is dyslexic.

Ignoring dyslexia as a myth.

3 DYSPRAXIA

Sam seems more clumsy than anyone else. Could it be a problem?

Description

Dyspraxia is an impairment or immaturity of the organization of movement. It is also known as Clumsy Child Syndrome or Development Coordination Disorder. School-aged children with dyspraxia avoid PE and games, react to all stimuli without discrimination, have a poor attention span, have difficulty in copying from the blackboard, write with difficulty, are unable to remember instructions and are poorly organized. Their handwriting is poor and they have difficulty catching a ball. Keeping balance and making complex movements is difficult. There may be little understanding of concepts such as 'in', 'on', 'in front of', etc.

There is a lot of overlap between the signs and symptoms of dyspraxia and dyslexia; research suggests that 52 per cent of children with dyslexia have features of dyspraxia.

Cause

It seems that there are undeveloped pathways between the two hemispheres of the brain. This lack of coordination in the brain exhibits itself in clumsiness by the child, whether in fine motor movements, balance or conceptual tasks such as jigsaws or creating charts and graphs.

Action

A diagnosis of dyspraxia may first depend on a teacher suggesting referral to a GP who may in turn refer on to specialist agencies.

Recognize the difficulties and allow for them but continue to encourage balancing, catching, fine motor activities, etc. in the hope of improving the underdeveloped brain pathways.

Help the child with organizing their day. Give them timetables for their bag and their bedroom wall, with clear signs marking what equipment is needed for each day.

Allow them extra time. Where possible teach in small bursts, allowing the chance to rest, if necessary. Provide worksheets to supplement whiteboard writing.

Pay more than usual attention to whether they have understood what they have been taught.

Priorities

Identification, diagnosis and referral.

Avoid stigmatizing pupils with dyspraxia by treating them significantly differently, but allow for the fact they may be slower and clumsier.

Alternatives

Use ICT to allow children to learn at their own pace. Emphasize the importance of drafting – putting down thoughts first then working towards accuracy.

Avoid

Stigmatizing a pupil by treating them significantly differently.

Being overprotective of pupils who bump into things and fall over.

4 ATTENTION DEFICIT/ HYPERACTIVITY DISORDER (ADHD) (ALSO KNOWN AS ATTENTION DEFICIT SYNDROME (ADS)

A boy in my class gets up and runs wild for a few minutes each lesson. Does he have ADHD and what can I do?

Description

ADHD is a medical condition characterized by overactivity, inattention and impulsiveness.

Cause

A chemical imbalance means an ADHD child can't process information in the same way as other children. For them, as the *British Medical Journal* describes it:

> The outside world rushes in with a flood of noise and images.
> The child cannot decide what's important and gets confused.

So the child finds it impossible to organize daily tasks and to see activities through to the finish.

Action

The two main treatments for ADHD are stimulant drugs and a talking treatment called behaviour therapy. Ritalin and Dexedrine can help the child concentrate, feel calmer and think before acting.

Keep a check on the child's behaviour in class, how calm or active they are at different times of day and you may find you get the best of the child's attention a short while after taking their medicine. You may find the worst behaviour as it begins to wear off. Be prepared for both scenarios and vary your expectations accordingly.

Priorities

Gaining access to appropriate treatment.

Remembering that the child's behaviour is not wilful but governed by a chemical imbalance beyond his control.

Minimizing the effects of the child's distracting behaviour on other pupils.

Varying classwork according to the child's capabilities at that stage in the illness.

Treat the child as a kinaesthetic learner and give him/her active learning tasks.

Alternatives

Parents can be encouraged to look at the whole child and investigate the effects of vitamin and mineral supplements; special diets with supplements such as fatty

苦

acids and vitamins; complementary and alternative treatments including visual exercises and biofeedback.

Avoid

Punishment for wilful behaviour.

Value judgements of good and bad behaviour.

5 GIFTED AND TALENTED

A child seems to be much brighter than the rest of the class and I don't know how to deal with him.

Description

Identifying gifted and talented pupils is not as straightforward as you might expect. Sometimes these pupils deliberately underperform or show behavioural problems in order to conform to peer pressure. There are many definitions of 'gifted' and 'talented'. This QCA guidance builds on the work of Excellence in Cities (EiC) which identifies

- 'gifted' learners as those who have abilities in one or more subjects in the statutory school curriculum other than art and design, music and PE;
- 'talented' learners are those who have abilities in art and design, music, PE, or performing arts such as dance and drama. (Excellence in Cities initiative)

In addition they are defined as in the top 5–10 per cent of pupils in a school.

Ability will not be confined to academic assessment, but could include the ability to solve problems, think quickly and creatively, be particularly sensitive or empathetic, be outstanding leaders, be fascinated by a particular topic or range of subjects, or be able to learn using an extensive range of strategies.

Cause

There is no single cause for those who are gifted and talented. Intensive learning regimes at home can produce apparently gifted children though this may be exhibited in a narrow range of skills, typically mathematics or music, but a gifted child can have a natural gift in almost any area.

Action

Systematically observe and identify gifted and talented pupils in a variety of situations, noting how they react, learn and perform relative to average class abilities. Look out for initiative, creativity and ingenuity.

Invite pupils to reflect on and talk about their own strengths and interests, leading to jointly setting personal achievement targets.

Talk to other teachers, parents and others who see the child outside school. Do they also see the talents you have observed and do they apply to a wide range of activities?

Provide resources suitable for a range of abilities and activities. Encourage learners to choose their own resources and to take responsibility for their own learning.

Priorities

Provide opportunities for children to extend themselves and realize their own potential, sometimes by additional work but often by providing choices of activity.

Provide a variety of learning activities to extend all learners' skills in diverse learning styles.

Use open-ended questions to stimulate creativity rather than closed questions and tasks with a predictable conclusion.

Alternatives

Celebrate diversity and talent in all children.

Offer group work where teams need to employ the skills of all the members.

Avoid

Stereotyping. Gifted and talented children shine in a diverse variety of ways. A bright, middle-class child with interested parents may be just that, not necessarily 'gifted' or 'talented'.

Creating the impression that the child is odd or peculiarly different.

6 AUTISTIC SPECTRUM DISORDERS (ASD)

A child in my class behaves very oddly. Could he be autistic – and what do I do?

Description

ASD describes disorders known previously as autism, Aspergers' and other names. It is thought that some form of ASD affects 1 per cent of the child population in the UK. Some children with ASD have a different perception of senses; they may have unusual sleep patterns and behavioural problems; they may have difficulty communicating and interpreting social situations; they are likely to interpret social language literally; they may behave inflexibly and grow distressed if routines are changed.

Cause

ASD is a neurodevelopmental disorder and is strongly genetic, though there may be environmental factors such as illness during pregnancy.

Action

Observe, identify and refer to a parent, then a GP, if ASD is suspected.

Assure yourself of the child's routines and reactions.

Play to the child's strengths, which may be the ability to concentrate for long periods on small details, technical or ICT-related skills rather than oral communication.

Because ASD children usually have unique learning styles, observing the ways they learn most effectively will usually help to structure their learning needs.

Priorities

Make instructions clear and literal.

Identify clear, short- and long- term goals with the school, the child and the parents.

Alternatives

Try to develop communication and social skills in the child, both at home and at school.

Avoid

Interpreting the child's behaviour as 'bad' or 'naughty'.

Teasing or joking, especially where the child is the butt of the joke.

7 GENERAL MEDICAL NEEDS

A child needs regular medicine taken in school time. What should I do?

Description

Some children have medical needs which require medicines and procedures during the school day. It is important to assure yourself that these are safe and approved, by conferring with the doctor, and that the school makes allowances to normalize these activities so the child is not treated as an oddity. Special training may be necessary to administer injections, which a teaching assistant could carry out if there is no nurse available.

Cause

So long as the condition does not adversely affect other pupils, the cause of the illness need not be a concern, though if the child needs special allowances then it is sensible to explain this to all the children. However, confidentiality should be observed if it is requested.

Action

Look at the issues of

- confidentiality;
- record keeping;
- the storage, access and disposal of medicines;
- home-to-school transport;
- on- and off-site activities.

Consult parents, the local authority and health services on all these issues and draw up an agreed action plan.

Consider whether and how far the child can be responsible for his/her own medication, perhaps kept in a fridge by the school secretary and self-administered under supervision.

Priorities

A plan agreed by all parties detailing when and how medicines are administered, whose responsibility it is at every stage, who to contact if there are any concerns. Teachers are not compelled to administer medicines but any volunteers should be appropriately trained and be assured of professional indemnity in the event of alleged negligence.

Alternatives

Invite parents to come in to school and help administer medicines.

Consider self-administration, with suitable safeguards.

Avoid

Letting the medical needs of a single child adversely affect the whole class.

Letting the child's medical needs drive his/her own school experience.

Overcompensating for medical needs.

8 ALLERGIES

I'm told that a child has allergy problems but I don't know how to handle this.

Description

Allergic reactions can take place with all manner of substances, particularly foods and animals. Some can be alarming, making breathing difficult or causing pulse to race (e.g. anaphylaxis, see below) but can nevertheless be coped with in schools with the advice of parents. It is very rare for people to experience extreme reactions.

The vast majority of allergies are mild and inconvenient rather than needing emergency treatment and manifest as a red skin rash, mild swelling or watering eyes. Asthma can be the result of allergies.

Cause

The general causes of apparently increased allergic reactions in young people are hotly debated, but the fact is that many children's immune systems do react adversely to particular foods and there are basic steps school and parents together can take to avoid or alleviate the situation.

The most common food allergies are to egg, fish, kiwi fruit, milk/dairy products, peanuts, sesame, shellfish, tree nuts, wheat. As ingredients of processed foods may contain a mixture of products there is always a chance of contamination. For example, Worcestershire sauce contains fish products, many processed foods contain traces of nuts and some dishes are cooked in sesame oil.

Hay fever is an allergy to pollen which causes watering eyes, a runny nose and sometimes wheezing. Some children will be best advised not to spend long out of doors during the time of high pollen count. This is typically May and June but differs according to which specific pollen creates the allergy.

Action

Every child should have a medical record available in school describing medical conditions, situations to avoid, doctors to contact. Make sure this information is provided by parents and kept up to date by the school. In an emergency it must be readily available, accurate and able to be acted upon.

It is sensible to distinguish on the medical record between minor and major allergies and for staff to be made aware of any serious reactions likely in pupils they teach.

The best line of defence is by the child him/herself avoiding the stimulus. However, the school needs to be aware of alerting children to anything which may cause a problem and must in particular label school lunches.

In the event of a reaction in any child, check whether you are aware of any known allergies, if there has been a known recent contact with that substance, and tell the emergency services. If the child has an Epipen for adrenaline, use it – preferably administered by a trained person.

Priorities

Information. Do you, the school and the child know what to avoid – and what to do if there is a reaction?

If in doubt contact emergency services and be ready to describe the known allergy.

Alternatives

Include lessons on hygiene, nutrition, cookery and food preparation and product labelling within the normal school curriculum to show how allergies are part of some people's everyday lives and how they can be coped with.

Avoid

Scepticism. Allergies are physical reactions, not social choices.

Banning certain foods throughout the whole school for the sake of an individual sufferer.

9 ANAPHYLAXIS

Emma is allergic to nuts. What might happen?

Description

Children can have allergic reactions to many substances but anaphylaxis is the most extreme form of reaction with anaphylactic shock being the most extreme and life-threatening form. It is estimated that 1 child in 70 is allergic to peanuts so the chances are that there will be at least one susceptible child in your school.

A serious reaction in an allergic child can be identified by significant difficulty in breathing or swallowing, sudden weakness, steady deterioration.

Cause

Extreme reaction to substances, especially peanuts, which the body's immune system regards as an invader.

Action

If there is an extreme reaction, this is an emergency. Adrenaline must be injected immediately and emergency services called. Injection will be either by Epipen or Anapen and the child and/or a volunteer member of staff should be trained in how to use this.

Administer the adrenaline while the child is lying down with knees up. The child should remain lying down and not under any circumstances stand or sit up suddenly.

Priorities

Avoidance of nuts.
   Identification of allergy.
   Administration of adrenaline.
   Call an ambulance.

Alternatives

Education of all children of the reasons for and consequences of nut allergies.
   Include lessons on hygiene, nutrition, cookery and food preparation and product labelling.

Avoid

Foods containing nuts. Bear this in mind if holding a multicultural day where children might experience some foods for the first time.

Foods most likely to contain peanuts or tree nuts include cakes, biscuits, confectionery, veggie burgers, salads and salad dressings, pesto sauce and Indian, Chinese, Thai or Indonesian dishes. Marzipan and praline are both made with nuts.

10 DIABETES

Amy has to have snacks during lessons for diabetes. What's it all about?

Description

Diabetes is a condition in which the amount of glucose (sugar) in the blood is too high because the body is unable to use it properly.

Hypoglycaemia (Hypo) is the situation of having low blood-sugar levels.

Schools can be in a position to notice the signs that a child may have diabetes. The main symptoms are:

- increased thirst;
- going to the loo all the time;
- extreme tiredness;
- weight loss;
- blurred vision.

Cause

Most children will have Type 1 (insulin dependent) diabetes.

Most children with diabetes will be treated by a combination of injected insulin and a balanced diet, plus regular physical activity.

Action

Make sure that meals and snacks are eaten at regular intervals to maintain the child's blood glucose levels. It's important to know when snacks need to be taken so you can monitor them and perhaps make sure the child gets to the front of the lunch queue.

Priorities

Identify hypos by warning signs including:

- hunger;
- sweating;
- drowsiness;
- glazed eyes;
- pale skin;
- trembling or shakiness;
- headache;
- lack of concentration;
- mood changes, especially angry or aggressive behaviour.

If a hypo occurs, treat it quickly by bringing glucose to the child in the form of a sugary drink or a spoonful of honey or jam, followed up by a sandwich, cereal bar or biscuits.

In the unlikely event of the child losing consciousness, place him/her in the recovery position and call an ambulance, saying the child is diabetic.

Alternatives

The child should eat before taking strenuous physical activity.

If staying overnight on a school trip, the child will need to take insulin injections and monitor blood-glucose levels. You should be confident that the child is able to do their own injections or that there is a member of staff who is willing to take responsibility for helping with injections and blood glucose testing.

Avoid

Hypos, by monitoring symptoms and checking that regular eating takes place.

Having the child use diabetes as an excuse for not taking part in physical activity.

11 ASTHMA

Ben wheezes and coughs in class, especially after PE.

Description

Asthma affects one in five households in the UK. It is a condition that affects the airways causing breathing difficulties.

Asthma attacks rarely happen without any warning. Sufferers get to know what triggers their asthma attacks and use peak-flow meters to estimate how effectively they are breathing. Most users carry inhalers to alleviate the condition.

Hyperventilation, on the other hand, which can be mistaken for an asthma attack, occurs typically through overexcitement and is associated with panic attacks.

Cause

Asthma can be caused both by genetic and environmental influences. A family history of asthma and eczema may lead to asthma in children and so may smoke, household dust and atmospheric pollution as well as contact with domestic animals.

Action

If there are mild symptoms these can best be treated with an inhaler.

If no inhaler is available, contact parents.

An asthma attack may display any of the following symptoms:

- cough, breathlessness, wheeze or tight chest get worse;
- the child is too breathless to speak, eat or sleep.

In which case:

1. Use the reliever inhaler (usually blue), immediately.
2. Sit but do not lie the child down and loosen any tight clothing.
3. If there is no immediate improvement during an attack, have the child continue to take one puff of the reliever inhaler every minute for five minutes or until symptoms improve.
4. If symptoms do not improve in five minutes – or you are in doubt – call emergency services.
5. The child should continue to take one puff of the reliever inhaler every minute until help arrives.

Within 48 hours of an emergency asthma attack the parents should make an appointment for the child to see a doctor or asthma nurse for an asthma review.

Priorities

Use the inhaler first, then call a doctor if it doesn't work.

Alternatives

Excitement or distress can cause hyperventilation which could be mistaken for an asthma attack. If the child does not have a history of asthma, suspect hyperventilation. Either way a prevailing sense of calm will help.

Avoid

Panic.

12 PANIC ATTACKS

Sam breathes in a panicky way if he's under stress.

Description

Hyperventilation occurs typically through overexcitement or anxiety and is associated with panic attacks. It can cause dizziness and a rather frightening shortness of breath.

Panic attacks also cause sweating and heart palpitations.

Asthma sufferers are normally aware of their condition and carry reliever inhalers, but panic attacks can happen without warning.

Cause

In hyperventilation, the body has too much oxygen. It feels short of air but in fact it has too much. To use this oxygen the body needs a certain amount of carbon dioxide.

Panic attacks can come about by being associated with fears from previous occasions. Seeing a dog could remind a child of a previous attack by a dog and the symptoms recur. A variety of phobias can generate panic attacks.

Action

Try to calm the child down. Use soothing words and tone of voice. Take the child to a quiet place away from the source of the panic, if it is known. Use a medical room if you have one.

For hyperventilation do the following three things to rebalance the oxygen intake:

1. Have the child hold his/her breath for 10–15 seconds at a time. Repeat this a few times until the breathing pattern settles down.
2. Have the child breathe in and out of a paper bag, if available.
3. Tell the child to take a brisk walk or jog while breathing through his/her nose.

Priorities

Keep the child calm.

Regularize breathing.

Alternatives

Taking regular aerobic exercise should relieve stress and avoid hyperventilation.

Try to determine the source of the panic so it can be avoided or so counselling can take place.

Avoid

Treating an attack as a crisis. You'll only increase the tendency to panic.

Confusing hyperventilation with an asthma attack.

As teachers taking care of our pupils, we need also to take care of ourselves. In the end we have more influence on our pupils by setting a good personal example than by any academic knowledge we may have.

1 TEACHER EXHAUSTION

I'm constantly exhausted and can't teach as well as I want!

Description

Work is tiring, but teaching can be exhausting. The combined demands of preparation, administration, performing for an audience and being eternally on show create a stressful situation. Add to this the pressure of having to be the life and soul of the party at Christmas (end of the longest term) and at the end of the summer term (end of the year) and it has been fairly compared to struggling to keep upright in an unstable boat in the middle of a white-water torrent, avoiding pointed rocks, while trees are being hurled at you. All the while trying to keep smiling.

Cause

Teachers are by nature (or were when they started) enthusiasts. They like to put everything into their work. This is why they are such bores at parties and why they run themselves ragged until the last day of term before they go down with flu. Wearing yourself out being lively in front of a class then working till midnight is immensely praiseworthy, but is counterproductive.

Action

Pace yourself. This doesn't mean being lazy. It means making the most of your energies.

To boost energy, reduce alcohol and coffee intake and maintain a healthy diet.

Keep fit, whether at a gym, cycling to work or taking an evening walk.

Get a good night's sleep, regularly, if not every night.

Aim for a good work–life balance to include time for family and time with friends.

Ensure at least one night a week and one day of the weekend are work free (leave that school bag behind!). Try to get a break at lunchtime and only work through lunch if it is to make the evening free.

Don't stay late at school every day, especially if you arrive very early.
Evaluate and prioritize your work:

- What must be done *now*?
- Why?
- Will you or your pupils benefit, or is it an arbitrary deadline?
- What is the worst that will happen if you don't do it now?
- If you do it now, will it make your life better tomorrow?

Note that work expands to fill the time available – and don't let it.

Take note of the tendency to work harder even when the increased benefit is slight – and aim to stop before that point.

Note that hard work is not necessarily good work – 'work smart, not long'.

Priorities

Pace yourself.

Identify what is essential and immediate and what is optional or unnecessary.

Reserve your energies.

Take time to relax and switch off. Identify what helps you do that and regard it as a treat to indulge yourself.

Alternatives

The alternative, not doing this, is to become ill, bad-tempered and to impose that bad temper on your friends, family and pupils as well as yourself.

Devise work avoidance (not evasion, that's different) strategies such as planning in advance a work-free night, recording it in your diary and ostentatiously leaving your bag at school.

Develop alternatives to written work (peer marking, oral work, drafting, etc.) to avoid the heaviest marking burden.

Save, file and retrieve your lesson plans so you can improve and reuse them (where relevant!) instead of reinventing them annually. Try to implement this in your school so there is more sharing of plans and resources between teachers.

Avoid

Working for the sake of it.

Trying to fight the pain barrier of sore throats and sickness.

Energy-depleting extra activities.

2 UNIFORM

Inspecting their uniform takes so long I can't get on and teach!

Description

Where sweatshirts and polo shirts have replaced jackets and ties, enforcing the wearing of uniform is not the curse it once was, yet it remains a permanent irritation.

The natural rebelliousness of many teenagers can focus on the apparently petty uniform restrictions. This in turn causes arguments which can disrupt the learning process and sour the relationship between teacher and pupil.

Cause

The arguments go something like this:

For

It encourages conformity – we appear to be heading in the same direction.

It provides a necessary discipline.

It is a symbol of pride in one's school.

It acts as a lightning conductor for rebelliousness – if the rebels are railing against uniform they are less likely to be stirring things up elsewhere.

It evens out social class, rich and poor, as they all wear the same uniform.

It simplifies the daily choice of clothes.

It saves money relative to expensive fashion clothes.

Uniforms of one form or another are common in the workplace.

Against

It can be an extra expense for hard-pressed families.

It can be a focus for bullying by pupils from other schools.

It encourages a rigid conformity, irrespective of shape and size, which is unnatural and unfair.

It can be a focus for hypercritical teachers.

Petty uniform rules distract from learning.

A particular cause of breaking the rules is the way fashion introduces a way of reinterpreting the rules. For example short skirts may be worn legitimately if there is no mention of skirt length in the rules. Amend the rules to state a minimum length and in due course fashion will bring about long skirts which again need a reinterpretation of the rule. The same goes for shirt colour; shirts worn outside trousers, or with T-shirts or football shirts underneath; tie colour, length and knot; sweatshirt colour, worn with or without jumpers or shirts; coats, hoodies worn in class or around the school, concealing a lack of uniform . . . the list is endless. I have personally attended a staff meeting dedicated almost entirely to the Great Problem of White Socks, and as for shoes versus trainers, don't get me started . . . .

Action

Ensure school rules on uniform are known by all. If it's an issue for you, have a copy pinned up on your classroom wall (and check it regularly so that no one defaces or rewrites it).

The rules should be readily available, clear, reasonable and unambiguous.

Sanctions if the rules are broken should be equally clear and the school and parents must support teachers in this.

Enforce the school rules on uniform just as you would for any other rule.

Appreciate that enforcement must be consistent and reasonable.

Staff should agree on the extent the rules may be interpreted. How do you deal with scruffiness and untidiness? With make-up and jewellery?

Priorities

Keep calm. Don't become a martinet.

Be fair and consistent. Make sure you are equally firm with girls and boys, able and less able.

Get on with teaching and learning as soon as possible.

Alternatives

Make a note of transgressions in pupil day books and ask for proof that their parents have read it.

Make an obvious note of uniform transgressions, sending copies to parents, tutors and keeping one for report-writing time and parents evenings.

Younger children may respond to charts and star competitions for the neatest class.

Avoid

Believing that every other teacher allows this or that (whatever pupils may say).

Ignoring the issue in the hope it will go away.

Getting it out of proportion – you're a teacher not an outfitter or a sergeant major.

3 ENCOURAGING GROUP COHESION

My class doesn't seem willing to work together . . . .

Description

Every class you teach is a group, but not every class either knows the other members or is prepared to work together. This is particularly true in large secondary schools.

Individual teachers can do a lot for the school as a whole by ensuring pupils know and respect each other. That starts in your classroom and continues on to the playing field, the playground and into extra-curricular activities. Inter-form competitions of all kinds create friendships between pupils, and if the tasks vary – running and ball games but also classroom decoration, fund-raising, even litter collecting! – give the opportunity for a child to shine and to build relationships with others.

Cause

As pupils enter your classroom they may have an identity in your eyes. They are, after all, stamped with the same label – Year 7 English, group C or whatever, and they are therefore a group. Soon they will have their own identity – the quiet lot, the restless ones . . . . However, ask each pupil about the other members of the class and they may know little, if anything, about each other. Why should they? It's up to you to mould them as a group: to enthuse the quiet lot and direct the energy of the restless lot to creative ends.

That won't happen until they see each other as individuals with personalities and something to offer.

Action

When learning pupils' names, make a game of it and take the opportunity of learning more about them. Push a balloon to a pupil (or a *very* lightweight ball) and call out their name; he/she responds by saying something positive or interesting about him/herself before passing the balloon on.

When arranging activities, vary the groups. This gives people a chance to find out about each other. Make the activities group tasks where individuals can shine and others can remember them for positive contributions.

Devise activities around revision of previous work. This simultaneously gives the chance to check prior learning, fill in gaps that may have been missed when pupils were in separate classes in the previous year and leads the class in to a new year with relative confidence.

Invite feedback from each group and vary the choice of the reporter so more people have a chance to be seen.

Use pupil names in class whenever possible. In the first week or two ask the class to introduce themselves or talk about themselves, even if for only 15 seconds.

Priorities

Activities developing group cohesion are more important in the early days of your class than assessment or new teaching.

Knowing pupils' names and at least one relevant fact of interest gives you a way of establishing a relationship.

Alternatives

Praise the class where possible.

Refer to them positively if a guest or another teacher comes in to the room.

Invite other teachers in to the class to see their excellent work so they may praise them too.

Do this only if it is justified, but look actively for examples of success.

Avoid

Saying, 'You ...' or pointing, when using a name would be more personal, friendly and professional.

Saying, 'You are the worst class I have ever ....' I have heard this often, and it is almost certainly untrue. It is unlikely to encourage pupils to make more positive efforts.

4 SUPERVISORY DUTIES

Why do I have to stand around when I've got more important things to do?

Description

Supervising children is a very important job. Not only because of health and safety and the duty of care but because it places you in a responsible position on public view.

Cause

A cause of irritation is likely to be that you have to rush from teaching a class to supervising an area of the school with barely a break. The sensible and practical option is to be prompt but give yourself a few moments to leave your teaching resources and pick up a cup of coffee on the way.

Action

Treat your duties conscientiously.

When you are there take a prominent position so you can see and be seen, even if your mind is elsewhere.

Take this as a learning opportunity and the chance to build relationships with pupils outside the classroom.

Start conversations with pupils. Ask them about themselves, what they think, their likes and dislikes. A straw poll on the new uniform, lunchtime arrangements or the school buses can help you in staffroom debates and in your teaching.

Priorities

Be prompt.

Be seen.

Act professionally.

Be prepared to leap into action if there is a fall or a fight – and move to forestall incidents by good-humoured encouragement rather than harsh discipline.

Alternatives

If a particular duty does cause problems, talk to the Deputy responsible immediately you realize. Don't take unilateral action first. Any sensible manager will appreciate you can't do any early morning duty if you have child-care issues or long journeys to school. Do be flexible and willing to take an alternative, remembering it's rarely actually going to be convenient for anyone.

Avoid

Missing a supervision. You place yourself in a position of neglecting a duty and put extra pressure on other colleagues.

Becoming embittered about standing in the rain waiting for buses to arrive. Store that up to complain to the coach company!

5 STATUTORY DUTIES

Is there no end to the things I have to do as a teacher?

Description

There was a time when a teacher had to do any 'reasonable' task the Head required.

As a result of a review into working conditions, the School Teachers Pay and Conditions Order of 2003 is much more specific about what is and is not required.

- A teacher employed full time must be available for work for 195 days in any school year, of which 190 are days on which they may be required to teach pupils in addition to carrying out other duties.
- Teachers are required to be available for 1,265 hours in a school year, during which they may be directed to perform duties by the head teacher. Any directions must be 'reasonable'.

The Pay and Conditions Order states:

> In carrying out his professional duties a head teacher shall have regard to the desirability of teachers at the school being able to achieve a satisfactory balance between the time required to discharge his professional duties and the time required to pursue their personal interests outside of work.

The Order also states that 'a teacher shall work such reasonable additional hours as may be needed to enable him to discharge effectively his professional duties' but these hours 'shall not be defined by the employer'.

There are 21 tasks listed in the Order which should no longer be the responsibility of teachers. These include administrative and clerical tasks, exam invigilations, and cover for absent colleagues beyond 38 hours per year.

Ten per cent non-contact time is assured.

Cause

If you do feel that what you are being asked to do flies in the face of the national agreement, then your recourse is first to the Head, then your union representative and thence to the union itself. But take note of the weasel clauses about what is reasonable and about discharging effectively your professional duties.

Any definition of a professional incorporates an individual's decisions about the standard of work and the amount of time taken to complete it effectively. Imposing time limits moves us away from professionalism and into clocking on and off. There have to be limits, and the best are self-imposed, leaving due time for a personal life, but still striving for high professional standards.

The 2003 Order helps define that space but cannot impose it.

Action

Check what the Order recommends.

Consider if what you are required to do contradicts that.

If you feel it does, ask yourself if you are doing more voluntarily or if more is being imposed upon you.

If the former, consider your own work–life balance. If the latter, talk to your Head.

Priorities

High professional standards within a fair work–life balance.

Be proud of the standards you achieve.

Alternatives

Either take another job with time limits or accept the situation and seek satisfaction in your work.

Avoid

Bitterness and resentment.

Clock watching.

6 DRUG TAKING

I think one of my pupils is taking drugs – what should I do?

Description

Behaving erratically and having dilated pupils may be signs of drug taking, but they may equally be signs of adolescence, late nights and trouble at home. Teachers are in the first line of identifying drug taking but have a duty of care for the pupil, whose best interests may not be served by publicity surrounding a drug-related incident yet may need professional help.

Cause

Possession of and use of certain drugs is illegal. Some drugs are open to abuse by overuse and some contravene the school rules. The dividing lines between these are not always clear, so great care should be taken when dealing with a suspected drug-related incident lest it get out of hand. Confidentiality is important. The Head may decide not to reveal to police the name of the pupil or pupils involved.

Action

Syringes

If a child brings a used syringe into school, first remove the syringe, being careful not to injure yourself. Then check whether the child's skin is broken. If there is a sign of a skin puncture, contact parents and get medical advice.

Then find out where the syringe came from and inform the Head and parents.

Smoking

If a child comes to school smelling strongly of smoke try to find out whether this is the passive result of others smoking at home or whether the child has been actively smoking.

If the smoking was off the school premises you need take no further action. If smoking was on the school premises, refer to the school's drugs and smoking policy and inform parents.

Drinking alcohol

It is an offence to buy alcohol under the age of 18, though depending on where and how it is consumed (in the home with parental agreement, or on licensed premises with a meal) it may not be an offence to drink it. The Licensing (Young Persons) Act 2000 created a new offence, known as 'proxy purchase', of purchasing alcohol on behalf of a person aged under 18 years old.

If drinking took place on the school premises, refer to the school's drugs policy and inform parents. If the result of drinking was inappropriate behaviour, deal with this in the usual way and withdraw the child from the classroom. Police should be informed if the alcohol was acquired by 'proxy purchase' or if the alcohol was sold illegally by a retailer.

Finding illegal drugs

If you find something which you believe to be an illegal drug on school premises, remove it, if possible with a witness, and place it in a locked drawer. Make a note of the incident and its time and place and tell the Head, who should then have the police remove the substance, check what it is and investigate where it came from.

Parental concern about possible drug taking

Make sure you have genuine reasons for believing this. Consider the confidentiality of this information and the possibility that if the child becomes aware of your concern they may react adversely. If any incidents have taken place on school premises you must act in accordance with the school's drugs policy. In any event you must act in the child's best interests. It is wise to record the incident, to check as best you can whether there is a real concern, which may involve questioning the accuser and the accused separately.

Any search for unauthorized substances should be done in the presence of a witness.

Supplying of illegal drugs on school premises

This can include sharing of drugs between friends even if no money changes hands.

Investigate the incident, speaking individually to each person involved. It may be better to wait until the individuals are calm. Invite parents to attend. Make a record of the conversations. Explain school rules on the subject.

Confiscate the suspect substances and have that witnessed.

Consider whether the police should be informed.

Priorities

Act in the child's best interests.
Maintain confidentiality.

Alternatives

Explain to the child the dangers involved.

Ensure the school's drugs policy is effective and up to date.

Ensure PSHE lessons deal effectively with the subject and that all pupils attend these lessons.

Avoid

Being judgemental.
Scaremongering.
Acting without evidence.

7 HARMFUL OR INAPPROPRIATE BEHAVIOUR

I think one of my pupils is harming herself.
A pupil seems unnaturally vicious and seems to hold power over another pupil.

Description

Behaviour such as self-harm (cutting an arm with razors), inappropriate sexual behaviour in public (which may harm the adolescent themselves or others) or unusually aggressive manipulative or threatening behaviour are often symptoms of deep unhappiness and may be the result of suffering abuse from others. The child should be considered a child in need.

In assessing whether the behaviour is unnatural for this age group, consider how many of the following are evident:

- Is the behaviour legal?
- If carried out between two or more people is there a significant difference in age, size or authority?
- Is there true, non–coercive consent?
- Was force used with or without anger and aggression?
- Was there a degree of secrecy?
- Have there been complaints?
- Are there any sadistic or ritualistic features?
- Is the behaviour a one-off or persistent and is it escalating in degree?

Cause

Self-harm is usually a symptom of low self-esteem. Unnatural sexual practices may come from personal experience of abuse or some other trauma.

Action

Do not be judgemental. Treat the child as a child in need.

Refer the child's behaviour to your school's counsellor or social services. The sooner these behaviours are identified the easier they are to resolve.

Priorities

Refer as soon as possible to your school's counsellor or social services.

Note that the police also offer child abuse services.

Alternatives

Ask the child for an explanation of the behaviour. This should only be done in a non-threatening way and if you are confident of a good reaction.

Make the Childline service and phone number available to the child. This may be done inconspicuously and without being directly aimed at the child.

Avoid

Alarmist attitudes when this may be a single uncharacteristic action by an unhappy, but not disturbed, adolescent.

Using vocabulary such as abuser or sex offender.

Trying to take on responsibility for this behaviour without training.

Talking about the behaviour with the child alone and in private. Disturbed children with sympathetic adults are prone to fantasize and to fabricate stories involving you.

8 BEREAVEMENT

A child in my class died on a school trip this week – how can I best talk to the rest of the class?

The mother of a child in my class died recently. How can I best support the child?

Description

Deaths at school or on school activities naturally require emergency services at once.

Deaths by members of the school – teachers or pupils – happening out of school hours can be no less traumatic.

Deaths in the families of pupils require a different approach.

Schools can provide a focal point for mourning, a source of accurate information and a reassuring presence.

Cause

Death or injury on school premises requires a close look at the school's and the county's policies. Attribution of responsibility is important and can lead to blame if failures are found. However, 'accidents do happen' and it should not be presumed that there is anyone to blame.

Action

Deaths at school or on school activities

Implement first-aid procedures. Move other pupils away from the scene and care for them. Call emergency services immediately.

Contact immediate family using the pupil's contact details and give these to the police too.

Get accurate information to the people who need it. Inform the Head, chair of governors and local authority.

Express genuine concern and a caring attitude.

Say you are sorry (this is unlikely to later suggest you were responsible or guilty).

Talk about the special qualities of the person who has died.

Reassure that the care given was the best possible.

Break the news to pupils. Make sure it is accurate and truthful. This is usually best done in small or class groups, especially in familiar and secure surroundings rather than an assembly.

Consider bringing in bereavement counsellors for other members of the school to talk to.

Follow this with a range of flexible activities so counsellors and teachers can move among the children and talk to them according to their needs.

The activities should help re-establish the normality of the school day.

Concentrate on the positive memories you have of that member of the school – 'What we remember best about him/her was ...' but it is not necessary to forget the person's weaknesses too.

Prepare an assembly for later, to inform, reassure and commemorate. Include parents and governors in the commemoration.

Provide opportunities for children to remember the dead person, by compiling an album of memories, writing stories, songs and poems or writing a letter to them.

Dealing with bereavement in the medium term

A child returning to school after a family bereavement needs care for some time after the event. Friends of a dead child need similar care and consideration.

Acknowledge and support their grief.

Accept that grief is expressed in different ways and show it is natural to feel sad and to cry.

Avoid euphemisms such as 'passed away' or 'gone to sleep'.

Children need reassurance that death cannot be caused by negative thoughts, sayings or bad behaviour.

Make some allowances for changes in behaviour while a child is upset, but do not abandon the usual rules.

Priorities

Provide reassurance, accurate information and a sense of normality.

Realize that reactions to bereavement can themselves be distressing, but usually follow a pattern from shock and disbelief, denial, growing awareness to acceptance.

Bereaved people may experience yearning and pining, anger, depression, guilt and anxiety and these emotions may be aimed at themselves or at others.

Alternatives

Include bereaved children in normal school activities.

Consider creating a commemorative plaque, a bench, part of a garden or planting a tree to remember the dead person.

Share concern and understanding with the parents too.

Avoid

Letting your own sense of helplessness keep you from reaching out to a bereaved person, whether child, parent or teacher.

Ignoring the bereaved person because you are uncomfortable. They may feel your actions isolate them even further.

9 CHILDREN WITHOUT FRIENDS

Brendon is a lonely and isolated child. How can I help him?

Description

Some children are naturally solitary, so we shouldn't assume that everyone wants to join a gang, but school is a socializing place as well as a place of learning and teachers have a role in encouraging friendships and cooperative activities.

Someone is bound to be a Billy-no-mates for a while and this will pass, but a teacher can arrange things quietly so the lonely one meets suitable friends.

Cause

Children's early home life will affect their ability to socialize. The number of children they have met and played with, whether they went to playschool or kindergarten, the number and age of other family members and neighbours, plus their own and their parents' inherent characters will tend to make them more or less at ease with others.

Action

A teacher has some responsibility for socializing a child.

We can do this by grouping pupils together and changing those groups according to ability and activity.

Look out for isolated children and introduce them, without fuss or bother, to others.

You may allocate a buddy to a new pupil to ensure there is always someone they can turn to.

You may change groups around so pupils meet a variety of others, but keep an eye on those who seem lost without a particular friend.

Peer-support groups are groups of pupils who volunteer to look after and help those in trouble, who need help or are isolated. With some training they can be excellent guardians and counsellors. Members of peer-support groups usually learn a good deal about themselves as well as helping others. They need careful teacher guidance but the all-round benefits are significant.

Look out for genuine opportunities to praise the isolated child. Appropriate praise will improve the child's sense of self-worth and cause others to think more highly of him/her.

Consider jobs which the child will see as a privilege and not a punishment, and which will be genuinely helpful to the school without being detrimental to the child's schooling. For example, making TV recordings, tidying tables and store cupboards, sharpening pencils, organizing PE kit, gardening, acting as host or messenger in the school lobby.

Priorities

Socialization and integration.

Observation before action.

Genuine praise where possible.
Adjusting groups.

Alternatives

Giving responsibility is a good way to raise someone's profile. Being in charge of pencils or the class library helps provide a self-identity.

The school library may provide a safe haven for a child prepared to help tidying and organizing or taking a duty on the loans desk to free up the librarian.

Avoid

Imposing too much.
   Showing up the child as different.
   Always letting children choose their own groups.
   Becoming the child's only friend.

Like it or not the computer is now an essential tool for teaching and learning. You don't need to be a genius but you do need to be able to cope with breakdowns and present a reasonably confident front to the class.

1 CHECKING FOR THE RIGHT EQUIPMENT

I'm constantly losing pens and books I give out to the class. Where am I going wrong?

Description

Some schools judge the success of a teaching practice by the number of pens or books the student teacher has lost in a term. In other schools giving out equipment isn't necessary at all. Certainly having to start a lesson by counting out basic writing materials is a problem.

Cause

The climate and routines of the school affect whether pupils bring their own equipment or depend on the school for it. The teacher also influences this by tolerating forgetfulness and carelessness or by enforcing rules about basic equipment.

Action

First, find out what happens in other classes. Do other teachers have stocks of pens, pencils and paper? What do other teachers do when faced with a pupil without a book?

Next, decide on whether you're going to follow the crowd or stake a claim. It will be hard to be the only teacher who refuses to loan pens or who will not tolerate 'forgotten' exercise books but it may be feasible with a new incoming class.

If possible, and if you are not alone, aim for firmness in dealing with this issue. Confirm the school rules on the subject, explain your very reasonable requirements to all your classes and explain what sanctions you will impose if a pupil transgresses. Be prepared for a fight and stand firm, especially with older pupils who may have become used to a lax regime.

If individuals 'forget' exercise books regularly, record the events with dates and take the issue first to the form tutor and then if necessary to parents. Add comments in day books and reports.

If the problem is giving out school equipment and not getting it back, ask the science and design and technology departments how they cope. Consider numbering text books, compiling pupil lists and recording which number book they are given. If necessary, have pupils sign when they take and return each book. Make a big thing of this and write to parents if you can be certain the pupil has failed to return something promptly. Write a standard letter in advance which explains the likely sanctions (extra work, detention, compensation payment, etc.) and can be quickly sent to the pupil's home.

Consider making wooden blocks with drilled holes to store pens or pencils. These provide a visual check of how many items have been returned.

At least in the early stages of this regime leave plenty of time before the end of the lesson for missing items to be returned. Make a fuss if anything is missing. Have everyone look for missing items and stand until they are returned.

While you should have a spare pen for genuine emergencies, such as for someone whose pen has broken during the day, consider offering a pencil instead, with the requirement that any work done in pencil must be written up in pen in time for next lesson.

Record all warnings and sanctions in your register. This will be valuable evidence in the case of future arguments.

If textbooks are provided for examination courses, consider insisting that pupils who fail to return them, or library books, will be fined and/or *in extremis* will not receive their examination certificates.

Priorities

To enable the lesson and learning to take place without delay.

To ensure the return of school equipment.

To have pupils assume the responsibility for their own equipment and therefore their own learning.

Alternatives

Include list of basic equipment requirements in a letter home to all parents at the beginning of the year.

Have form tutors check kit and record this in day books which parents must sign.

Organize a small stationery shop in the school selling writing implements and mathematical equipment.

Raise the profile of the humble pencil case. Use it to provide source material for art, English and language vocabulary. It's surprising how well you can carry out an intelligent conversation based on the vocabulary of items in a pencil case!

Avoid

Pupils relying on you for spares of everything.

A climate of carelessness.

2 NETWORK DOWN! ELECTRICITY OFF!

I've organized a great lesson but the network's down and now I can't teach it. What do I do now?

Description

If you are about to teach a lesson which relies on the school network for resources, communications or software tools, the cry of 'Network down' can strike fear into you. Your plans are thwarted, you have to find an alternative.

Cause

Electrical failures, essential maintenance, pupil interference, server hiccups and lightning strikes can all cause the network to be unavailable. If you were relying on the network for your lesson, you have to think again, and fast.

Action

The first thing to do is to check that the network really is unavailable and that it can't be restored within minutes. Your network manager/technicians are probably already working on this but it is useful to check whether it is repairable in minutes or hours.

For small hiccups you can probably keep talking for a few minutes. Talk about the consequence of digital failure across the globe and its effect on the economies of the Western world – or pupils'computer games. Also talk about the consequences of not saving your work and backing it up. Describe scenarios in which all the children's own data files – coursework, assessment grades and timetables disappeared in an instant. What would be the consequences if it happened? How should we avoid that? Teach the unavoidable fact that we can't afford to rely entirely on computers. But what alternatives are there?

In any instance when it's unlikely that the network will come back on stream soon, go straight for your back-up plan. Your back-up plan is based around talk and various activities using rough paper and pens.

Your back-up plan could be:

Class discussion

- 'What would we do if all the computers in the world caught a bug and died?'
- 'There will come a time when the computers will control the people. Has it started already? How might we prevent it?'
- 'Who wants to be a cyborg (part man, part computer)? What could you do that humans can't? Is it something we should encourage or be afraid of?'

Paper-based tasks

- Design a website – your own or for a special purpose, such as for your year group. Consider navigation using menus, type styles, colours, graphics, content, purpose. Use a sheet of paper for each web page and draw links with clear arrows from one to another.

- Design unambiguous symbols for an online course. For example, what symbols would you create to describe assignment, deadline, essay, background reading, research, test ... ?
- Write a diary for an average day listing, describing and explaining how much ICT was involved (e.g. bills calculated, news delivered, emails collected, timetables created, worksheets and resources designed, library catalogue, supermarket checkout and your purchases saved as data, stock control and automatic ordering systems ...).

Priorities

Don't panic!

If you have a class to teach, teach them, don't faff about with cables and servers.

Once you've reported the network is down, leave the technicians to get on and fix it.

Alternatives

Always have a back-up plan. Never rely entirely on ICT.

If it's a teacher presentation rather than pupil access, do you have a copy on a CD or memory stick?

Avoid

Don't interfere or say, 'I wonder what would happen if I plugged this in ...'.

Don't let pupils mess about with the network.

Never get in the way of technicians trying to fix a network problem. Don't hover. Don't interrupt. Do bring them a cup of tea and some chocolate.

3 DATA LOSS

My computer crashed and I think files have disappeared! How do I get them back?

Description

You go to your computer or to your usual storage place on the network following a computer crash and find your files aren't there. At this point the situation is not a disaster, but it could become one if you do the wrong thing.

Cause

You can lose the most recent version of a file you're working on at the time of the crash or power cut, but even here automatic mini-saves should be operating in the background and a technician should be able to find the last saved version.

A crash is less likely to affect you if you're working on a school network. Networks are built with back-up procedures (yours is, isn't it?) so you can be fairly sure that, even if your main copy of a file has disappeared, there'll be a back-up copy somewhere safe.

The cause could be a virus, software bug, human error or hardware failure. If it happens on your standalone laptop or desk-top machine, tread very carefully as anything you do next could compromise the data permanently.

Breathe easier if you have a recent back-up copy. If you haven't, scold yourself and swear you'll make one immediately you get out of this disaster.

Action
School network

Check you are in the right place. Trace the route back to My Computer and My Network Places and see if you've ended up in the wrong area. Is this a computer you usually use? If not, it could be configured differently or the previous user could still be logged on. Log off and log on again. If that doesn't work, shut down the machine (using the Start menu, not the plug!) and restart. If the problem remains, contact your network manager or technician.

Standalone computer

If you can back-up anything to a memory stick or external drive, do so immediately.

If you can shut down the machine in a controlled way (using the Start menu, not the plug!) do so and restart. This may cure the problem on its own.

The best case is that you have everything backed up on an external drive, or at least your working files to a CD or DVD. The worst case is that your computer is out of action and you'll have to find a data recovery expert. Consider the (often considerable) cost of this in relation to the value of the data loss.

Use any data recovery software you have, strictly according to instructions.

Assess the situation using 'The Ontrack Data Disaster Scale' from www.ontrack.com

1. **File or email deletion**: a file or email is accidentally deleted or lost due to a virus.
    To do: check alternative folders, trash and any back-up files. Or, use self-recovery software.
2. **Loss of data on one computer**: a virus hits a PC or laptop and 'wipes' the hard drive.
    To do: check back-up, if available, run data recovery software.
3. **Physical damage to a PC or laptop**: computer is dropped, exposed to excess heat or water or caught in a fire.
    To do: do not try to dry, cool or rebuild the computer, or recover data yourself. Call a data recovery company immediately. However, a separate keyboard splashed with coffee may be retrieved by washing in clean water and drying out slowly. This is less likely to succeed if the cause was a sugary soft drink.
4. **Hard drive error:** computer reports that the hard drive is experiencing errors, and may be damaged or corrupted.
    To do: shut down computer immediately. The longer a damaged hard drive is left running, the more data that can be irretrievably lost. Call an expert, who will advise on next steps.
5. **Burnt-out hard drive or electrical circuit board**: part of the hard drive is damaged internally, due to age or power spike.
    To do: call a data recovery company.
6. **Physical damage or 'head crash' inside the hard drive.**
    To do: find the name and contact details of a data recovery company recommended by your hard-drive manufacturer and contact them immediately.

Priorities

Retrieve any available data as soon as possible and save it on another drive.

If the hard drive is making nasty noises, power down and shut down as soon as possible.

Don't overwrite anything on the broken drive.

Consider any action carefully before doing anything which could make the situation worse.

Alternatives

Work from your back-ups.

Put in place a regular back-up procedure. The easier it is to use the more likely you are to use it.

In future save regularly, especially before trying to print.

Ask your technician to implement automatic mini-saves at 15-minute intervals.

Remember that printed copies of your reports, worksheets and handouts may be available elsewhere. Hunt them out so they can be scanned in if necessary.

Remember that attachments of files you sent to others may still be available on their machines and, if you sent emails from other computers, you may still have copies yourself. Find them fast!

Avoid

Making things worse by precipitate action.

Overwriting your data.

4 INAPPROPRIATE WEB CONTENT

I found a boy looking at pin-up pictures.
I've been told that a girl has been sending bullying emails to other pupils.

Description

There is a great deal of material on the Internet which is inappropriate for young people. This may be sexual, violent or in other ways illegal or offensive. Remember that you have a duty of care for the child.

Cause

This is not simply an Internet problem. You should deal with the issue in ways which would be appropriate to any illegal or unsuitable behaviour in school.

However, the Internet has made inappropriate content more readily available than previously. Fortunately, the Internet itself can be filtered and blocked electronically to reduce the chances of inappropriate incidents. Any suitable Online Learning Platform should include measures to block content, check emails and trace incidents.

Action

Consider this as you would any illegal or unsuitable behaviour in school. Interview the child, refer to school rules, punish the child and inform parents as necessary.

If you see a pupil looking at an obviously inappropriate page, immediately switch off the *monitor* – not the computer – and move the child. Note the exact time of the incident and the user name of the child and tell the network manager or technicians immediately.

Look closely at your school's policy on Internet use. It should contain advice on what a child should do if unexpectedly faced with clearly inappropriate content, e.g. 'If you come across something you know to be unsuitable, which your teachers or parents would not approve of, move on rapidly to another page and inform your teacher immediately.'

Discuss with your network manager or technicians how this page became visible. They will be able to tell you the route taken by the child to that page and can test whether the school's Internet content filter was operating effectively.

Your ICT team should also be able to retrieve suspect emails and possibly even recall emails which have not yet been viewed. Bullying by email or by mobile phone usually leaves a data trail from which the bully can be identified.

Priorities

Take all action immediately before any traces are destroyed.

Interview the child and determine exactly what happened.

Ensure your Internet use policy is up to date and effective and that pupils, teachers and parents understand it. Ensure external chat rooms are blocked and that mail is filtered to eliminate spam and unwanted external contacts.

Consider making a public example of this incident to deter others.

Alternatives

Consider whether alternative Internet filtering services may be more effective. However, note that a filter can reduce but not eliminate the risk of exposure to inappropriate material.

Learning to use the resources of the Internet safely and appropriately is an important part of the education of all pupils. Make sure it is an integral part of the whole school curriculum.

Encourage use of the Yahooligans search engine rather than Google as it is more suitable for younger pupils.

If Google image search is used, ensure the Advanced Image Filter is set to Strict to filter out unsuitable pictures.

Avoid

Assuming that inappropriate content must have been searched for deliberately.

Assuming that Internet filtering is 100 per cent effective.

Assuming that no incidents will occur – or have occurred – in your school.

5 SHOWING VIDEOS AND DVDS IN THE CLASSROOM

I want to show a DVD in my PSHE lesson but I'm told some parents disapprove. What should I do?

Description
Your duty of care to the child, your responsibility *in loco parentis* and your desire to offer interesting and stimulating teaching material could be in conflict here.

Cause
A pupil may say nothing at the time but when parents hear what their child has seen (or what the child *says* he/she has seen) they may object. They have every right to do so.

Action
Be cautious in choosing your teaching material.

The British Board of Film Classification says that although a school may show *extracts* from a film of a particular category to children below the suggested age range, this is not recommended if the film contains material unsuitable for children younger than the age specified. Content should always be properly discussed and presented in an educational context. Seek parental consent prior to the screening if there is any doubt.

It is always important to make sure that any children watching the video/DVD are not likely to suffer any ill effects as a result of seeing the film.

Priorities
Check the British Board of Film Classification (BBFC) category marked clearly on the video/DVD. If there is no packaging, suspect this is an illegal copy and proceed no further. If it is a genuine tape/disk, check with the BBFC's website search for the classification.

A brief summary of the classifications system:

U   suitable for 4 years and over

PG   viewable with parental guidance but should not disturb a child aged 8 or over. Some scenes may be unsuitable for young children

12   suitable for 12 years and over

12A   no one younger than 12 may see a 12A in a cinema without being accompanied by an adult

15   suitable for 15 years and over

18   only suitable for adults

R18   only to be shown in specially licensed cinemas.

Obtain the approval of the Head, governors and parents where there is any doubt at all. Explain your educational reasons for showing the film.

Alternatives

Use something less contentious.

Choose sanitized extracts and make these brief. Consider editing the film to cut out contentious scenes, filling in gaps with a summary and continuing to the next section.

Avoid

Being persuaded by a vocal few in your class that this horror movie/teenage escapade is entirely suitable.

Showing anything which is likely to disturb children.

Showing anything brought in by pupils unless you have watched it yourself, checked its classification and are assured that it is acceptable.

6 CONFISCATING BELONGINGS

Do I have the right to take away a pupil's mobile phone if it rings in class?

Description
A pupil's mobile phone or music player is disrupting class work. Some schools permit phones and electronic equipment, some do not. You should not tolerate ringing during lessons. Nor should pupils be sending or receiving text messages.

Cause
Any disruption of lessons can be dealt with using existing school rules and policies. An occasional classroom incident where the phone rings because it was accidentally left on may merit a warning, but repeated infringements may reasonably require confiscation. However, it is the teacher's judgement whether confiscation would solve the problem or make it worse during a given lesson.

The government White Paper of 2006 is reported as saying that teachers will be given the right to confiscate pupils' mobile phones or music players if they hinder learning. Many schools will already have made this possible through their own school rules. Some commentators believe confiscation goes against human rights legislation.

Action
Give general and specific warnings in advance: 'I want you all to check now that your phones are off. If any phone rings during this lesson, I warn you now that I will confiscate it.'

Ensure that school rules are clear on the issue and that parents are informed in advance.

Incidents should thereafter be treated as would any occasions of disobedience.

Confiscate and keep safe. Put the item in a secure place labelled clearly with the date and the owner's name. Write immediately to parents explaining the reasons for confiscation and the conditions under which the item may be returned. Some schools require a parent to come to the school and reclaim it in person, following an explanation of the school rules.

Priorities
Ensure that learning continues uninterrupted by electronic bleeps and squeaks.

Ensure that discipline is maintained – pupils switch off phones if school rules or teacher request demands it.

Ensure that pupils and parents know what is accepted and what is not – and the likely action that will be taken if the rules are broken.

Note that 'disrupting other pupils' learning' and anything on health and safety grounds such as continued loud music on headphones are good reasons for confiscation. Advising pupils not to bring in expensive items because the school cannot ensure their security is simply good advice.

Alternatives

Warnings are preferable to confiscation.

In the first instance confiscated items may be returned at the end of the school day if the pupil collects them and promises that this will not happen again.

Offer to look after the mobile if the parent insists the child needs it for medical or personal reasons.

Avoid

Becoming irrationally angry, especially if you can't identify the culprit because it rings only once each time.

Losing or damaging the confiscated item (and that includes using that phone or iPod yourself).

PART 6 RELATIONSHIPS

Teachers are often confined to classrooms, cut off from the continuing small interactions with other adults for an hour or so at a time. Sometimes we feel staying in the classroom to supervise, tidy up or prepare is more important than keeping in touch with colleagues. However, that contact is an important part of the school community and helps everyone to help each other. None of us is as good as all of us.

1 WITH OTHER STAFF

How do I meet people when I'm in a classroom all day?

Description
While in most workplaces there is time throughout the day to talk to colleagues, teachers are mainly trapped in classrooms. Lunchtime and break may involve duties, last-minute preparations or long-distance moaning sessions. Meetings have business or pupil-centred agendas. In these conditions relationships with other staff can be difficult to create or maintain.

Cause
Surrounded everywhere by pupils or their imminent presence, by the paraphernalia of teaching and with education as the main topic of conversation, it's not surprising that a teacher's social life is limited.

Action
Arrange a get-together after work. Try very hard to talk about something other than work. Consider inviting a few non-teachers too – and that includes caretakers, cleaners and office staff.

Arrange a regular activity with like-minded colleagues – badminton, circuit training, football, an interdepartmental rounders match (but share out the PE teachers), a cricket team, a quiz team.

Hire a coach for colleagues and spouses, and consider selected governors and parents too, for an evening play or concert.

Priorities
Get to know people you wouldn't normally see in your day.

Work together as a team.

Gain mutual respect – and friendship – by your honesty, willingness to listen and help.

Alternatives
Even baking brownies or bringing in biscuits or chocolates to break time helps group cohesion. Providing a subsidized meal before a parents' evening makes the evening more congenial.

Avoid
Too much solitariness and isolationism.

Cliques. There's a fine line between a cohesive group and an antagonistic clique.

2 IN THE STAFFROOM

As a new teacher I feel a bit lost in the staffroom. How should I behave?

Description

The staffroom is seen by some as the centre of the school, where teachers share information, discuss issues, mark work and plan teaching. This may be true in some places, but in a school with a long-established staff it can also be a room where a fixed hierarchy operates, where certain chairs are allocated for life and where close-knit groups rehearse oft-repeated old tales. The dynamics of the staffroom affect the whole school whether it is a small primary school or a large secondary school, so it is difficult to generalize.

Cause

A new teacher can find it off-putting entering a staffroom where established groups and behaviours are in operation. Making a first impression on any new group is important and an early faux pas can take some time to be forgotten. In a large and busy staffroom maybe no one will notice you; in a small and friendly room you may be warmly welcomed.

Action

Look before you leap. Follow others and note what they do in terms of conversation, respect, coffee or tea (choice, pouring, paying, tidying up after) and seating. If in doubt, hover. If possible, join up with a more experienced colleague for a while.

Don't sit until you have been either invited or you have worked out where the sacred areas are.

Come to school prepared with loose change to pay for coffee or tea.

Determine beforehand what is usual for lunch. Later you can make your own mind up whether to eat your own sandwiches in the staffroom, join the children in the dining hall (check if there are free lunches for supervision duties and what these consist of) or run off to a local deli.

Listen – carefully and widely. A good staffroom is a learning opportunity. You can hear wondrous tales of erratic pupils and eccentric teachers doing outrageous things, which put your own experiences in context and from which you can learn to be a better teacher.

Priorities

Think before diving in.

Be prepared with small change – and if in any doubt offer to pay immediately.

Make friends widely. You are part of an important team.

Ask for help and be grateful for it, though don't feel obliged to follow it.

Alternatives

Some secondary school departments have their own bases where they hide or prepare at break and lunchtime. This makes for more departmental bonding but less whole staff cohesiveness. Spending some time in both areas makes for a good balance and helps integrate you into the school.

Avoid

Attaching yourself too soon to an established group. The group may appear interesting and welcoming but could be viewed negatively by others.

Hiding alone.

Spending too long in your own classroom instead of mixing with the staff.

3 STANDARDS OF PERSONAL BEHAVIOUR

I've experienced teachers who are kind, sympathetic and intelligent; sometimes I'm bad-tempered and irritable. How should I aim to behave?

Description

Some would say, 'To thine own self be true' while others would say, 'Never smile before Easter.' In practice it has to be a balance between your own nature, remembering the reasons you wanted to be a teacher in the first place, tempered with a frown and a firmness which says clearly to pupils, 'I will not be crossed. Don't even think about it.'

Cause

The reason for asking the question is based on the commendable desire to be a good teacher, and the challenge of improving your own qualities to include both the velvet hand and the mailed fist. This may not come naturally to you, so you have to work to create the balance. Typically a young teacher is optimistic, generous and sympathetic to the pupils, then gradually learns the importance of defining limits to acceptable behaviour to prevent pupils taking advantage of them. In some older teachers the movement is the other way, towards cynicism and bitterness, possibly as a result of repeated efforts by pupils to take advantage of his/her better nature. In which case, it's time to go . . . .

Action

Look back at those who taught you and around at those you are teaching with. Who would be your role model? Or are there qualities in several people which you would like to adopt? Consider how and if you could emulate these people, and if you think it's possible, aim to do so.

Look at your clothes and hair, hygiene, stance, voice (and how tone, pitch and volume change according to what you are trying to communicate), regular phrases and sayings (do you call the pupils 'folks', 'chums', 'guys' or 'people'? do you know enough of their names to address them individually?), how you introduce and finish off lessons (is this lively and inspirational, methodical or routine?), and how you interact outside lessons (are you warm and friendly, energetic and sparky, cool and grumpy, tired and ratty?). Much of your behaviour has to be natural to you, but a degree of acting is valuable too.

Priorities

Behave in an 'enhanced natural' way.

Be kind yet firm.

Be professional.

Alternatives

Take acting lessons. Not to create a false persona, but to enhance the qualities you already have and compensate for any perceived weaknesses.

Take voice lessons to reduce the strain on your voice, increase the qualities of projection and develop variety.

Avoid

Trying to be someone who is certainly not you.

4 STANDARDS OF PROFESSIONAL BEHAVIOUR

I'm a different person in the staffroom, the classroom and when I meet pupils outside school. How should I behave?

Description

While there is naturally an overlap between personal and professional standards of behaviour, professional standards are described and codified by the General Teaching Council (GTC).

Cause

Because transgressions are notifiable to the police and a teacher may lose their job and their teacher status, it is vital that all teachers are aware of the behaviour required.

The leaflet 'Professionalism in Practice' by the General Teaching Council for Scotland makes this very clear:

> Legally a teacher is in a unique position of trust and therefore criminal behaviour which breaches that trust or is related to child abuse, child pornography or offences of a sexual nature are incompatible with being a teacher. (www.gtcs.org.uk)

Action

Read the professional code of the GTC, any similar code or advice produced by your professional association or union, and any additional code or policy produced by your school.

It will include, for example: areas of illegal conduct, including firearms offences, violent crime against a person or property, serious public order offences, theft, dishonesty, fraud or drugs offences. This will probably not include minor traffic offences, but these could be taken into account if they become serious or repeated.

The main areas identified by the English GTC are:

- demeaning or discriminatory behaviour;
- reasonable care;
- cooperation and collaboration;
- confidentiality;
- examination and assessment.

The Scottish GTC includes, among others, the following list:

A teacher should not:

- allow professional relationships with colleagues, pupils or students to be prejudiced by views about their lifestyle, culture, disability, beliefs, colour, gender, sexuality or age;

- allow behaviour with colleagues, parents or pupils to be affected by prejudice against gender, beliefs or lifestyle;
- swear at pupils or colleagues, or use offensive names;
- undermine the professional standing of any colleague by remarks which are malicious, unfounded or unprofessional;
- have in their possession at any time illegal or inappropriate; materials/images in electronic or other format.

A teacher should:

- conduct teacher/pupil conversations about sensitive issues discreetly;
- treat all colleagues fairly and in accordance with the law;
- be fully accountable when handling school funds;
- follow employer policies and procedures;
- be accurate and honest in providing information;
- guard against inappropriate workplace banter or practical jokes.

Priorities
Above all a teacher must be of good standing and trustworthy.

Alternatives
The only sensible alternative to behaving professionally as a teacher is to take another job outside teaching.

Avoid
Being unprofessional in any way.
    Breaking the law.
    Ignoring or transgressing the code.
    Believing the code to be sufficient. It is a minimum standard, and a high level of personal conduct will cause you to rise above this.

5 WHISTLE-BLOWING

A colleague seems to have close relationships with a small number of pupils. I can't prove anything is wrong but I feel uneasy.

Description

Staff working with young people are open to accusations of improper relationships. They also have to work closely with young people in a pastoral role which can involve discretion, and which may be misinterpreted as secrecy.

Whistle-blowing also applies to any poor practice or performance.

Cause

It is right that anyone who has a reasonable suspicion of wrongdoing by a colleague should be able to bring this to the attention of a responsible authority who can investigate whether there is anything unprofessional going on.

This does put a great responsibility on the whistle-blower, who may be wary of jeopardizing relationships within the school and may not feel they have sufficient evidence to prove their case.

Action

Consider your responsibility primarily to the children, but also to the staff and the school. How would you feel if you did not speak out and later discovered there had been improper activities?

Only you can decide whether the evidence you have is enough to raise a concern. If you do so you could prevent a problem getting worse, you could protect others and you will, incidentally, avoid yourself being implicated.

Your reasons for not speaking out may include the fear that you may not be believed, that this could have a bad effect on your colleagues and your own career, or that you may start a process that could spiral out of control.

There is a natural fear of getting it wrong – have you misread the signs, made a mountain out of a molehill, put two and two together to make five .... .

If you have reasonable grounds for your suspicions you have a responsibility to act. You do not have to prove your allegations but you do have to have reasonable evidence.

Talk to someone you trust and voice your concerns, trying to focus on exactly why you are suspicious. The earlier you do this the better. It may be that this will clear up the problem, but if you get an unsatisfactory response take matters further and put your concerns in writing.

Priorities

If your suspicion concerns children, your first priority is for the welfare of the child. Don't think, 'what if I'm wrong?' – think, 'what if I'm right?'

Second is loyalty to colleagues and the school. This loyalty is misplaced if there is real cause for concern.

Third comes the natural concern for yourself, your relationships and your career.

Consider this call from Barnados: 'Absolutely without fail – challenge poor practice or performance. If you ignore or collude with poor practice it makes it harder to sound the alarm when things go wrong.'

Alternatives

If your school, union or local authority has a whistle-blowing policy, read this before you act.

Consider carefully before sharing your concerns with colleagues generally. Rumours spread easily and get exaggerated; unfounded rumours, especially if traced back to you, will help no one.

Consider carefully before approaching the colleague directly. Will your approach prove your suspicions are mistaken or warn a guilty person and potentially implicate you?

Avoid

Acting single-handedly.

Doing nothing when you have a reasonable suspicion.

Acting maliciously.

6 WITH SUPPORT STAFF

How far is our hard-working caretaker a colleague like a teacher?

Description

Teachers are professional educators. That doesn't mean they don't need help from 'para-professionals' and other people who make up the greater school community. In fact a good school celebrates the strengths and variety of everyone who helps in a school. 'It takes a whole village to educate a child' should apply to the whole school and its community.

Cause

Unfortunately there is an elitism in some schools, where administrative or grounds staff are unwelcome in the staffroom. That elitism can pass on to the pupils, who may come to think of non-teachers in a condescending way.

Action

Include all staff – teaching and non-teaching – in general newsletters and staff photographs.

Start from the assumption of equality and provide all staff with similar pigeon-holes, email addresses and access to coffee-making facilities, lunches, car parking. If grounds staff, technicians, office assistants, caretakers, etc. prefer facilities more conveniently elsewhere or at other times because of their different jobs, that's fine, but they should not feel excluded from the staffroom or from general school news and events.

It is a wise school which uses the expertise of support staff to help broaden the curriculum, extend the life of the school into the community, help with disaffected pupils, vocational courses, etc.

Priorities

Establish your responsibilities at an early stage and build up a good working relationship.

Maintain some professional distance by observing confidentiality regarding other staff and pupils, especially if you are in a position of authority in the school.

Alternatives

Balancing a healthy appreciation for support staff, who are generally not well paid, with remembering that as teachers we hold the responsibility for pupils in our care can be a balancing act where the difference in roles is not appreciated. At times, some professional distance on the part of the teacher can help establish your respective roles.

Don't forget to thank support staff, who often work beyond the call of duty. While mutual help is considered to be part of the professionalism of the teacher, it should not be taken for granted in support staff and deserves genuine thanks when it occurs.

Avoid

Either condescension or over-chumminess. In other words, just be yourself!
   Taking support staff for granted.

7 WITH GOVERNORS

I'd like to be friendly with my attached governor but I feel self-conscious that they may be reporting back on me.

Description

An interested governor will want and need to talk to you about your work in the school to inform him/herself of the way the school works. If you can trust that person enough to tell them what you really think and they can take what you say in good faith, you can build a mutually beneficial relationship.

If you see this primarily as an opportunity to feed your grumbles into the system, or the governor sees you as a potential aid in some power struggle of their own, no one will gain.

Cause

Governors now have more responsibility for school matters than ever before. They have a huge influence on the way a school is run, setting key policies and helping to develop the school's vision, yet they are volunteers.

Their responsibilities include appointing the Head, salary setting and budget allocation and to do this involves liaising with the Head, teachers, parents and the local authority. They aim to monitor the direction in which the school is heading and strategically to steer it in that direction, with the cooperation of the Head.

In the circumstances it is not surprising that a teacher might find an interested governor simultaneously a welcome listener and a potential informer.

Action

Work with the governor over a period of time and decide for yourself how far you trust each other. Honesty on both sides will benefit the whole school though, as in any serious relationship, keeping some early reserve is wise.

Priorities

Offering an honest and open view of the school.

Alternatives

If your relationship with the allocated governor seems not to be working and you feel you cannot be open with them, talk to your Head about it. The Head may feel they can move governor roles around or quietly guide the governor (or you) towards a more effective way of working together.

Also search your own soul and ask yourself what you are wary of. Do you lack confidence in what you are doing or are you unhappy about any of the things the school is doing?

Avoid

Excessive criticism or self-praise.
Extreme reserve or chumminess.

8 WITH THE COMMUNITY

I live in the catchment area and find parents want to talk to me about school issues when I'm out of school.

Description

Living in the catchment area can be difficult. You are seen, known and judged. In a way you become public property.

Cause

On the one hand you need to know what issues the community has, but on the other hand you need space for yourself. This used to be called 'living over the shop' and while it was an indicator of commitment and good service you may find it's refreshing to get away from the day job. The notion of being The Village Schoolmaster or Miss Read is romantically appealing but can be a heavy yoke to bear.

Action

Weigh up the relative merits of travel, housing, being part of a community and getting away from the day job. Teaching is not a job you can easily cast off as you close the classroom door but it can benefit from understanding the community and being known. If you don't want to walk into a shop or a pub where your purchases and your appearance will be known to the whole school next day, move out of catchment and put up with a longer daily journey to school.

Be sure to discuss this with your nearest and dearest. Does your spouse want to be part of the community to this extent? Will your children attend the same school as you, and what is their view on that?

Priorities

Your effectiveness at doing the job.

Alternatives

Short of weekly lodging, your choice is between in or out of catchment. Do you live to work, or work to live?

If you decide to live out of the area, make an effort to involve yourself in some extra curricular or community activities.

Avoid

Having your life taken over by your job. Decide on limits to your day, have at least one night off every week and don't say 'yes' to every load that is placed upon you.

Living so far away that your daily commute consumes all your after-school energies.

9 REGARDING VISITORS

The Head is always asking me to host outside visitors and I feel I can't say no – but it's a burden I can do without.

Description

Local schools sometimes breed local visitors keen to show interest; successful schools often attract inspectors of good practice. However, visitors can distract from the essential task of teaching and learning and can become a burden on teachers already at full stretch simply coping with the class.

Cause

Popularity, success and a willingness to embrace the community are all reasons for including visitors. However, large numbers or frequent visits can destroy the atmosphere which made the school successful in the first place. Teaching which is interrupted by well-intentioned questioning, having to act as host during lunch and breaktimes or being viewed through windows as you teach can make you self-conscious and your teaching artificial.

On the other hand, the attention can be flattering, the visitors stimulating and integration with the community can bring unexpected rewards.

Action

Agree a quota or limit of visitors. You might hold an open doors community day where the focus for one day only is on demonstrating your achievements to visitors so you can then attend to your pupils the rest of the time.

Certainly limit the visits made to a particular class or teacher as this may not only affect them unduly but risks causing division among the rest of the staff if one teacher is being singled out for attention.

Consider giving teachers who host visitors extra non-contact time to compensate for the extra pressure. A small charge could be made for some of these visits which could supplement the staffing budget or at least buy something which clearly benefits the school.

Priorities

Ensure teaching and learning are not compromised by the extra burden.

Ensure certain areas of the school, or particular teachers, do not receive undue attention.

Alternatives

Agree a quota.

Spread the load.

Make use of visitors to broaden the curriculum, provide a captive audience and actively take part in school activities where this will benefit pupils and yourself as a teacher. Have them judge a competition, listen to reading, talk about their jobs and their lives. Involve them where you can.

Avoid

Undue concentrated attention.

Extra load borne by less favoured parts of the school.

The Head hogging the limelight and receiving praise which should rightly go to individual teachers.

10 BETWEEN THE MANAGEMENT TEAM AND CLASSROOM TEACHERS

I have recently been promoted and a colleague jokes that I now seem aloof and distant with colleagues. Could she be right?

Description

It's not unknown for colleagues aspiring to management jobs to dress in smarter suits and act rather more seriously than previously. Some people feel they have to show they've taken on more responsibility by becoming more distant. To those who know them this may seem a contrived change.

Cause

Management responsibility may bring the need for a positive public face and necessarily comes with responsibilities, both collective and personal. The difficult balancing act is remaining a good friend with colleagues while holding a little in reserve. That distance and reserve gives you the space to keep some matters confidential, to observe situations in an even-handed way and even to be a critic of others' performance if necessary.

Put simply, it's easier to caution a colleague about their slack marking or lateness if you're not their close friend.

On the other hand a manager who holds him/herself aloof may fail to appreciate the problems his/her colleagues are having and may lose sympathy by appearing superior.

Action

Consider that promotion may be easier to cope with by starting afresh as a new broom rather than being elevated within one's own school.

Ask yourself how much you want to be liked and how much you want to run a tight ship. Doing both simultaneously is possible, but not easy.

Be sensitive to the distance you must maintain in order to do your job professionally. That distance will vary according to the size and characteristics of the school, its staff and your own sociability. However a Head or Deputy significantly affects the ethos of a school and being too chummy or too severe will influence the school's atmosphere, and ultimately its success.

Establish yourself for your genuine merits. Experience, personal skills, creativity, being a very good teacher, being well organized and working as an effective leader of a good team will earn you respect worth far more than the artificial respect accorded to one of the management.

Priorities

Being good at your job.

Positive personal relationships with the whole school community.

Alternatives

It is possible to hide away and do the paperwork or the relationships with external agencies while leaving a Deputy to represent your public face. Equally you could appoint secretarial staff to do the bureaucracy while you put yourself around the school, and mix with staff and pupils. Neither is ideal, though having faith in (and praising) your staff while taking ultimate responsibility for their actions is a mark of a good team leader.

Avoid

Being aloof.

Imagining you deserve respect simply because of your position – or your suit.

11 WITH PUPILS

Description

Relationships with pupils need to be professional and caring but not too close. You are their teacher, not an uncle and *never* a sexual partner. This should be obvious, but from time to time there are well-publicized liaisons between teacher and pupil. A few are discreet and do not proceed too far while the two parties are at school. However, some are highly inappropriate, unprofessional and break the bounds of acceptability.

Where there is any question of a teacher having undue influence over a pupil leading to sexual relations, this is bound to lead to dismissal and to inclusion on List 99 of adults banned from working with children.

Cause

Adolescents can be attractive, naive, yet have considerable power. Teachers can be the victims of teenage crushes and can be flattered by the attention. The fact that such a relationship is taboo may even make it more secretive and more appealing.

Action

Sixth-form pupils are frequently attractive and lively. They may admire and desire a friendly teacher. All the more reason for the teacher to keep a professional distance. This may mean not being in a room alone with them and will of course mean no physical contact. It means avoiding social meetings unless there are chaperones such as other teachers or a larger group.

Younger pupils naturally see a teacher as a help, a parent substitute, if they are hurt or otherwise need help. Sadly, male teachers of young children need to take the greatest care here as any suggestions of paedophilia can ruin the teacher's life.

Priorities

Maintaining appropriate relationships while supporting pupils.

Avoiding any opportunity for anyone to hint at an unprofessional relationship between teacher and pupil. Where there is scope for misunderstanding, your career could be on the line.

Alternatives

Some teachers marry people who were once pupils at their school, which is fine, but any suggestion that the teacher 'influenced' the pupil are still likely to be frowned on.

Avoid

Avoid sex with pupils. Full stop.

Don't mix work and school. Don't invite pupils home. Don't touch pupils. Don't get into situations where any of this is possible. Be a teacher, not a partner.

12 WITH PARENTS

I'm more terrified of facing parents for five minutes than I am of the class for an hour!

Description

Meeting parents to discuss their children can be a daunting experience.

You are in a position of professional authority, so greet them cordially, make absolutely sure who you are supposed to be talking about and start with a résumé of achievement based on marks and grades and backed up by observations and examples.

Cause

Parents, perhaps accompanied by their children, may come with an entirely unexpected agenda and you must be prepared to deal with that or at least to commit to pass the issue on and report back on progress. The more information you have at your fingertips, the better.

Action

There's more to assessment than marks, so broaden your assessment to skills and abilities generally. Make notes of this so you can narrate personalized events and examples of behaviour and attainment.

Priorities

Summarize achievements.

Make positive suggestions for improvement.

Invite comment from parents and listen to them.

Deal with any concerns.

Alternatives

Record any real or imagined concerns parents have and agree to act upon them or refer them on.

Collect exercise books and marked work to refer to if necessary. Poring over every piece of work will be too time-consuming for a brief appointment but it may be useful to refer to for specific cases.

Keep to time. Be prepared to bring the appointment to an end with a brisk conclusion and a smile. Also be prepared to sum up an excellent pupil with an enthusiastic but very brief eulogy; wise parents will beam and leave without the need for greater detail.

Avoid

Excessive detail.

Excessive generalities – especially when trying to hide the fact you don't know the child.

After the initial report, talking too much. This should be a two-way meeting.

Comments on the supposed failings of other teachers or the school in general.

Overrunning the time slot.

Work isn't everything – but sometimes it's hard to believe that. A work–life balance that enables you to do a professional job without sacrificing your personal life is an extremely difficult thing to achieve. Teachers are well known for being strongly focused on their jobs. And if you are aiming for a career in teaching you may be looking beyond being a full-time classroom teacher. These are stressful pressures which need firm plans and maybe even strategies for getting out altogether.

1 WORK–LIFE BALANCE

Work is taking over my life!

Description

The *2003 National Agreement on Pay and Conditions* says that all teachers should enjoy a reasonable work–life balance. It is the responsibility of the head teacher to ensure that staff have an appropriate workload, having regard for their health and welfare.

A balanced life is a happy life. Having interests outside school makes you a better teacher and a better person. No one ever said on their deathbed that they regretted not spending more time at the office. But pressures of work are considerable. They come from the amount of work, the desire for pupils to have their work marked, the school's desire to reach the highest standards and from you to do your best. But there's more to life than work.

Cause

Do you work to live or live to work? Probably a bit of each. Work pressures in schools are more intense than in many work environments. The desire to do your best for yourself and for the children, the drive to forge a career, the intensity of lesson after lesson with 30+ children in your care, the accumulation of responsibilities ... all add up to a job which dominates your life.

Sometimes the other side of your life doesn't get a look in. There's little time in the school day to think about home and family or yourself. When you get home you're tired and irritable and if you do go out socially you tend to be thinking about work-related issues.

Sometimes a focused work session can blot out depression caused by other factors – but this can only be a short-term answer, like a pain-killing pill. Sometimes an intensive work session is needed to clear the decks, and that can be liberating, but you may have only tackled the immediate problem, not the root cause.

Action

Allocate time for yourself, friends and family.

You can do this by creating fixed boundaries such as a minimum of one night each week when you leave early, come what may. If you have to work on a Sunday preparing for the week, make sure you keep Friday night and Saturday completely free.

Lobby for one weekday to be kept free of after-school meetings.

Take up an out-of-school interest which has no connection with your school work. And beware – badminton or running or gardening can so easily slip into becoming a school activity too!

Setting firm boundaries around your personal life helps to keep school from taking over everything. It gives you the freedom to say 'no' to the next meeting and is a point around which you can plan your marking and preparation. Setting firm boundaries is not a dereliction of duty – on the contrary, it's a sign of commitment and dedication.

Priorities

Allocate time for yourself.

If you can't do everything that's necessary within the time remaining, question your workload, not your dedication.

Be good to friends and family.

If your workload is too heavy, either take the issue up with senior management or prioritize it.

Take up running, walking, sport or gardening – something that brings fresh air into your lungs and clears your head. You'll be re-energized and more able to see things clearly.

Alternatives

If your work balance is making you ill, leave. And make that a positive decision.

Avoid

Letting the toad work squat on your life (as Larkin put it).

2 PROFESSIONAL DEVELOPMENT

I've been stuck in the same job for a few years. How can I get on in teaching?

Description

'Getting on' means different things to different people, so be clear in your own mind which direction you might take.

Professional courses and in-service training take a number of different forms. In addition to day-long courses by training organizations, local authorities and professional associations arrange evening and half-day events. Informal participation in school life provides variety and useful experience.

Cause

Job application forms usually require a list of recent courses, though the nature of the form tends to ignore informal professional development opportunities.

Be sure to refer to participation in working parties, an active role in training days and consultation processes, taking on voluntary responsibilities within departments.

Getting on as far as headship requires a National Professional Qualification for Headship (NPQH). Contact the National College for School Leadership for further information. Also try to speak to a Head or Deputy who has experienced the course.

Action

Identify possible career paths, your personal preferences and ultimate objectives.

Survey possible actions you could take to reach those objectives.

Discuss these with senior colleagues, line manager, professional development/INSET coordinator.

Look out for relevant working parties to join, courses to attend, qualifications to study for and people to shadow. Being an assistant involves helping other colleagues, experience which will pay later.

Join groups of teachers who include teachers from other schools, and invite yourself to other schools to see how they do things.

Look at job advertisements, not only in your local area, so that you get an idea of what kind of jobs are available and, over time, come to a view of your preferred job.

Priorities

Gaining experience. Voluntary participation demonstrates a willingness to work and a sense of purpose. You will be able to talk knowledgeably about your preferred post.

Gaining insight, so you are confident in where you are going – and why.

Alternatives

Establish in your own mind why you want to leave. Could things be made better in your present school or will change bring the necessary boost?

Consider whether your frustration comes from teaching itself. Look at alternative careers. Teachers have skills which are highly rated beyond teaching – communication, training, people skills, organization, self-motivation and the ability to work unsupervised.

Ask for support from senior colleagues and advisers on visiting other schools. Investigate how other schools tackle the problems your school faces and write a report on the possibilities. This will give you broader perspectives and greater insight.

Avoid

Going for another job just because it is expected of you. While aiming for promotion is expected of high-fliers, it is not right for everyone. If you can get more satisfaction classroom teaching than taking on management responsibilities, concentrate on classroom skills and perhaps aim to be an advanced skills teacher.

Becoming stale – a piece of the staffroom furniture. A change you choose for yourself often brings new life, which both you and your pupils deserve.

Time-serving – being there just for the sake of it. Surely there's something better to do?

3 ADVANCEMENT

I enjoy my teaching but I want to have more of a say in the school.

Description

Often people see classroom teaching as the essence of education at first, then gradually move to more senior management positions where they can have a broader influence. Management responsibilities usually come at the expense of classroom teaching. Some people like that, others don't. Some finally come back to the classroom, having realized that's where the greatest influence rests!

Cause

Wanting to have more of an influence is a natural development for a classroom teacher who feels confident in the classroom and starts to look beyond it. It involves participation in the management of the school and those democratic structures that provide a place for a voice to be heard.

Action

Look to take part in working parties, management structures such as a head of department or academic planning group and any open debates about the direction of the school. You may also look to help arrange the student council, training days, becoming a mentor or INSET coordinator, or teacher governor.

Priorities

Being where you will be heard or where you can influence decision-making.

Alternatives

Politics. Political decisions have a strong influence over school funding and the curriculum. Some find they can affect education more from local government than from within the school; others argue otherwise!

Avoid

Practical but time-consuming tasks. They are useful and appreciated but don't influence opinion.

4 NEW HORIZONS

Failed to get a new job and don't know what to do next?

Description

Psyching yourself up for a new job, then failing at interview, can leave you frustrated and not knowing where to go next. It can also can help you make your mind up about what you want or don't want from your career.

Cause

Teaching jobs typically allow you little or no time to decide whether to accept or to refuse. They also appear overwhelmingly around April and May, giving you little time to choose and a tendency to apply for several at once. Failure at the end of May usually means a very limited chance of a job for a further year.

Action

To avoid the problem

Before you start serious applications, request details of interesting jobs and use them to test your attitudes. Try to determine what is the perfect job for you. Are you prepared to move or to commute; do you prefer large schools, small schools, private or state system, town or country; do its advantages outweigh the disadvantages of leaving your present post; do you want change, responsibility, more or less teaching time; does this fit in to your long-term career plan?

Discuss this with friends or a partner. From this compile a set of essential features and desirable priorities with which to judge a job. Then you are in a position to apply seriously.

To cope with the problem

- Request reasons for not being offered the job.
- Take feedback on the chin and deal with it.
- Act to correct omissions or clear up misunderstandings.
- Practise interviews with senior colleagues.
- Amend the content or appearance of your CV if necessary.
- Invite comments from trusted colleagues on your demeanour, dress, deportment or anything which could improve first impressions of you.
- Involve yourself in active and positive career planning.
- Take steps to advance your continued professional development by shadowing, attending courses, reading up on current educational issues, acquiring further qualifications.

Priorities

Choose positively and actively.

Alternatives

Either tell yourself that you're lucky to have the job you've got – and get on with it.

Or tell yourself that you're relieved you didn't get it because . . . and use that to help you in active and positive career planning.

Avoid

Accepting a job just because you've been offered it. Make it a positive choice.

Assuming the world owes you a job. It doesn't.

5 GETTING OUT

I've had enough! I want to get out – now!

Description
There will be times when the pressure, the people and the job get to you and you want to get out. This is all perfectly natural – but it doesn't mean that leaving the school or teaching is the best answer, either for you or the profession.

Cause
Despair over any part of the system can sometimes take the blame for problems in your own life. Consider whether the real problem lies with you, or your job. Don't blame the pupils or the secretary of state for your personal frustrations.

On the other hand if it really is the school or the job, you need to make a considered – not precipitate – decision over your next step. Talking this over with a partner or friend should help, but beware of teacher or non-teacher friends who have their own prejudices and opinions.

Action
Visit a careers counsellor. Undergo a psychometric test. Discuss the results, your preferences, strengths and weaknesses. Talk with the careers professional about what you might be good at and how to go about it.

For the time being continue teaching as best you can, while simultaneously researching alternative careers; pension, mortgage and other financial implications; potential for early retirement, redundancy benefits, etc.

Update your CV, top up your training, press your interview suit or invest in a new one, roam widely and make yourself ready for a new future.

Discuss your plan, when you have one, with a discreet senior colleague.

Priorities
Leave no stone unturned in your search for a suitable alternative.

Make your leaving a positive decision, not simply a reaction.

Don't jump until you have somewhere to jump to.

Keep your own counsel over your future until you are sure.

Alternatives
Remember that the skills of a teacher (communications, literacy, people skills, self-motivation, etc.) are greatly in demand in the workplace.

If the initial desire to leave has passed, consider whether it was temporary or whether it is likely to return.

Avoid
Rash decisions which leave you with no job at all. If you're going to jump, make sure you have somewhere to jump to.

PART 8 ADMINISTRATION AND ORGANIZATION

Dealing with paperwork may seem to be a distraction from your teaching but we all need preparation, resources and recording and assessment methods. Try to think that organization will support and improve your teaching. If you can get returns and replies back to the people who need them, you'll be making them happier too!

1 RECORDING

I've been asked for class marks but my records are all over the place!

Description

Recording the results of assessment is a necessary part of a teacher's life. What and how to record is more debatable. Accuracy and objectivity are hard to achieve. A busy lesson in a busy day does not lend itself to thoughtful or methodical recording and reliance on memory is risky.

Cause

One problem lies in deciding what and how to record. Traditionally this was in a hard-backed mark book though many use a loose-leaf file. Columns indicated assignments and dates and rows showed comments and marks. A combination of numbers or letter grades plus ticks and crosses recorded achievement and attendance. The book was usually private to the teacher but had to be revealed to senior colleagues if necessary.

Making records available electronically as databases and spreadsheets or modules in a school information management system, and more widely dispersed via a school network, virtual learning environment or the Internet, means that grades, their meaning and significance, the standards and features they apply to and the way in which they are entered have to be standardized. Omissions and anomalies are open to scrutiny.

Efficiently entered marks may give the illusion of objectivity but a great deal of marking is highly subjective.

Action
To avoid the problem
At the least, be sure to conform to school and departmental policy.

Check this policy covers what should be recorded and how it should be kept, saved or published.

Consider your own recording system.

- A neatly kept, hard-backed mark book may help you feel diligent but will it help you share your marks across the school?
- Entering marks on the school information management system may look efficient but how do you transfer marks from exercise books to database, and is this convenient?
- Does the school database allow for subjective comments as well as marks?
- What scope is there in your own recording system for qualitative as well as quantitative assessment?
- Can you easily record absence, late homeworks, incomplete work, behaviour issues, personal observations?
- Can you identify patterns and trends as well as objective marks and grades?

To solve the problem once it's happened

Focus on this task as a priority.

Collect together all the data you do have. This should include pupil exercise books, your mark book, printouts of data already recorded by you or by others and any other material you have including school absence records, your own diary and any unmarked work you can find.

Mark any unmarked work.

Consider re-marking existing work for several specific features – e.g. accuracy of content, spelling, grammar, presentation and other specific skills relevant to your subject. Award and record marks for each skill.

Set a simple relevant test to be marked by pupils in class time. Collect and record marks gratefully. Similarly, if you have no data on a particular skill, set a brief task which requires that skill and mark for that skill only.

Using a spreadsheet (more adaptable than a printed mark book) enter pupil names and any grades and assignments you can rely on. Try to fill in gaps with derived data and central data such as absences (check school records).

If pupils are using eportfolios, access work done in other subjects too if this can be assessed by skill. For example an English teacher could assess several writing skills using work done in a History class.

Consider converting grades into marks or vice versa.

Consider creating aggregate marks from several separate assessments to compensate for marks which are missing, i.e. for four different written tasks Bill has 60 per cent, 40 per cent, Absent and Incomplete; so his aggregate mark for 'written fluency' would be 50 per cent.

As some of this, especially massaging statistics, is poor practice and could produce misleading results, get back on track with a new marking and recording regime as soon as possible after this immediate crisis has passed.

Priorities

Marking work.

Recording marks and grades for assessment.

Noting and storing comments and observations for report writing.

Alternatives

Peer marking, self-assessment and group activities may not produce marks and grades of the kind required by your school information management system. Nevertheless, they are excellent educational opportunities. Consider having the whole class award grades for public activities such as class presentations and demonstrations and use this as an opportunity for explaining the standards required.

Regular short tests can be easily produced and marked in class by swapping with another pupil. They produce simple quantifiable marks that appear to be efficient assessments and rapidly fill up mark books.

Day books signed by teachers and parents, punishment books which are followed up, praise books written by teachers and pupils all provide the raw material for report writing.

Avoid

Fraud.

Over-reliance on subjective assessment and memory.

2 REPORT WRITING

I have reports to write and don't know what to say!

Description
Every child is different, and reports should be personal, but reports express a defined range of abilities and achievements. There is bound to be some repetition and you would expect an accurate observation to be echoed in several different reports.

Cause
Faced with a large number of reports to write, inspiration is likely to fail.

Action
Acquire a list of useful phrases for report writing. There are examples in my *100+ Lists for Teachers* (2005). Create your own list specific to the skills you choose to assess.

Refer to the notes, assessments and observations you make during your teaching (see 'Recording', above).

Refer to photographs and an accurate list of names to check you're writing about the right person (and spelling their name correctly).

Refer to any of the following categories: accuracy, enthusiasm, motivation, work effort, reliability, ability, progress, potential, behaviour, character, presentation, attendance, cooperation, social skills, participation, attainment, achievement, preferred learning styles.

Priorities
Write a personal and accurate report.

Make comments based on evidence and observation rather than impressions.

Provide specific suggestions for improvement rather than general criticism or glib banalities.

Alternatives
Refer back to previous reports if necessary, but remember parents and pupils are ideally placed to recall and compare.

Computerized report comment banks have their advocates but tend to be formulaic and stilted. While the school may require references to attainment targets, parents and children prefer personal comment about them as individuals to quotations from the national curriculum.

Avoid
Being insulting, emotional, sarcastic, vague or inaccurate.

Being so bland it's clear you don't know who you're writing about.

3 DEALING WITH ADMINISTRATIVE PAPERWORK

How do I deal with all the paperwork? – I need an office!

Description

Teachers with offices have a huge advantage here. Teachers without offices need to be strict in their approach to paperwork, or it will cause chaos. Administration and bureaucracy may seem a burden, but remember that some of it is essential to effective teaching.

Cause

Classroom teaching rightly takes priority but paperwork, whether external or internal mail, administrative or otherwise, needs to be dealt with efficiently for the school to function. Often it directly helps your teaching. Lacking an office, you will need to have space and strategies for filing, forwarding and retrieving documents.

Action

First find some space. You deserve space in the staffroom or department base but it may be hard to claim exclusive rights in a cramped place. A storeroom is a last resort but if it has a window it could be sufficient. A classroom has the great disadvantage that you, and possibly several others, teach in it! Children and teaching generally do not go well with administration. Nevertheless, if that's your only space, identify a table or desk, drawers, folders and preferably a filing cabinet with dividers.

A desk and filing cabinet offer workspace, storage of stationery and records, and a filing system that can cope with expansion and can be locked for confidentiality. Think about your routine tasks, jot down likely headings for your files and write folder labels for each heading.

The paperless office has proved to be an illusion, but a great deal of paper can be saved by doing admin tasks electronically. Where possible within the practices of your school use internal email and a common storage system. An effective intranet or school network will have storage for each department, confidential pupil records, personal storage space, assessment records, a school calendar and email. A bulletin board may inform staff about current and imminent news. If this system is part of a well-thought-out learning platform all facilities will be brought together alongside pupils' own accounts and teaching resources.

The effect of this may be to reduce paper but increase communication. In terms of dealing with the emails rather than the written notes and letters you may need your own laptop in your classroom, a terminal in the staffroom and perhaps Internet access (ideally broadband and wireless) at home. The decision then is yours whether or not you want to deal with admin from home and how much you let work invade your home.

Remember that electronic communications generally are more efficient, so long as users check their mail and bulletin boards frequently. Messages and their replies are saved, and can be stored, organized and retrieved with little effort and no space. The contents can be copied, reused, repurposed and circulated – all with no need for further space.

It helps to have a regular time and place for administrative work. The routine can make admin less painful and the regular place means you can store everything together even if you can't leave your 'pending' tray lying around.

Priorities

Deal with admin regularly and frequently.

Prioritize the tasks.

Aim to deal with each item only once.

Prefer electronic to paper.

Make one of four choices for each item:

1. Act on it.
2. Pass it to someone else to act on (but be selective – don't send to All!).
3. File it.
4. Bin it (and don't be afraid to do this if possible).

Develop a routine for collecting, dealing, storing and retrieving.

Alternatives

Consider a combination of routines for paper and electronic admin but choose electronic communications where feasible.

If you seem to be receiving multiple or redundant requests, consider going back to the originator and suggesting different information retrieval methods.

Consider the relative merits of scribbled notes, face-to-face communications, email, electronic forms, etc.

Avoid

Losing things.

Accumulating admin tasks till they mount up.

Printing out electronic files.

4 REDUCING THE BUREAUCRATIC BURDEN AT SOURCE

I'm being crushed by unnecessary paperwork – how can I stop it?

Description

Some bureaucracy is essential. Without it you'd have no salary, no capitation, no idea how many pupils are expected in which class for which courses ... .

Yet sometimes the weight of paperwork can seem to be overwhelming the teaching. Fortunately workforce reform has been agreed and a National Remodelling Team (NRT) has the job of carrying this out. Visit www.remodelling.org for more information.

Cause

Accountability is at the core of much of the paperwork teachers receive. Schools have to show parents and government they are doing a good job; local authorities have to demonstrate the community charge is being well spent and their employees are working effectively; government has to show its funding is being used wisely and its policies are effective. Teachers usually end up having to provide the answers.

But are teachers the best people to do this? If it takes them away from teaching, this may be counterproductive; but on the other hand they may be the best people to provide the answers 'direct from the chalkface'.

Action

First identify the burden. The NRT identifies four areas of administrative activity:

- those which seem not to relate directly to effective education;
- those which are carried out more often than necessary, inefficiently or in too much detail;
- those carried out by teachers but which could better be done by support staff;
- those which could benefit from the effective use of ICT.

Visit www.remodelling.org for more information and search for Toolkit. Then implement the most appropriate strategy for each type of activity:

- stop doing unnecessary things;
- redesign the way you do things to be efficient and effective;
- match personnel to activities – 'the best staff for the job';
- make best use of ICT.

Often the solution will be to employ or redeploy an administrative assistant.

Priorities

Do what is best for pupils.

Continue doing what is legally required.

Minimize inefficient use of resources.

Leave sufficient time within the school day for preparation, planning, marking and recording (PPMR).

Alternatives

Urge your Head to use support staff for specific tasks. Collecting money, entering and collating data and invigilating examinations can all be done by non-teachers more effectively.

Avoid

Irrelevant and burdensome tasks.

Letting the tail (bureaucracy) wag the dog (education).

5 A SUDDEN INSPECTION

Ofsted are coming this week! What can I do?!

Description

The trend towards shorter inspections with less warning is intended to take pressure off teachers. Nevertheless, panic usually sets in and it's best to make good use of the brief warning time you have to present yourself to the best advantage.

Cause

Even experienced and confident teachers get nervous at the prospect of inspection. However, the OFSTED Handbooks do not suggest teachers make any special preparations:

> On no account should inspectors ask for any particular form of lesson-planning.
> Inspectors must not do anything either before or during an inspection which would encourage teachers to prepare or plan materials especially for the inspection. [The lesson] should be judged by how it supports teaching and learning, not by any preconceived idea about its format or detail.
> Inspectors will not ... expect staff to create additional paperwork specifically for the inspection.
> (OFSTED)

Action

Check you have essential preparation complete and evidence of it available.

Know what classes and topics you intend to teach.

Know what resources you will need.

Show how this lesson or topic fits into the greater curriculum, especially how this lesson relates to previous and future lessons.

Show your assessments so far including any test marks, reports, marked work.

Show how you cope with differentiation, extending the more able and providing for the less able and those with special needs.

If possible, look over relevant school policies and refresh your notions of how your work fits in to the stated policies of the school.

Look at the inspectors' advice sheet covering areas which they might discuss with you and, only if it serves to calm your nerves, have a colleague or spouse give you a mock interview. Practise being serious, not flippant!

Priorities

Show you are competent and organized in teaching, planning, assessment and recording.

Show you have a good and effective relationship with the class.

Alternatives

There is no alternative to teaching a good lesson.

Remember that teachers are often their own most severe critics, so don't dwell on any mistakes you may have made because the inspector will be looking at your successes rather than your failures.

Avoid

Panic!

Behaving unnaturally.

Overpreparation.

6 TOO MUCH WORK

I've got work up to my ears and I don't know where to start!

Description

You start to panic when there is work everywhere and still more comes through the door. Panic means you either flit from one thing to another ineffectually or stare stunned at the pile as it grows.

Cause

Excess work is certainly a problem in itself, and there are times when things all happen at once. Adopt one of the strategies below when (though preferably before) it all gets too much:

Action

Strategy 1 – Delegate

This may already be the cause rather than the solution of your problems. If you have anyone to delegate work to, think carefully before you add to their burden. Shifting the load to someone already overworked doesn't really solve the problem. However, if there is a keen young colleague willing to gain experience this could be an opportunity for in-service training.

However, shifting the load back to pupils can be helpful. Set tasks which involve preparation and drafting. Set activities which involve discussion, reading and problem-solving and which can be assessed in class and don't add to your marking burden. Have pupils try peer marking and supervise their work in class.

Strategy 2 – Time shift

This means putting off the inevitable to a time when you may be more free of immediate pressure. Setting a project which won't be handed in until the end of term so you can mark it in the holidays may feel good now but you may regret it later. Secondary teachers tend to believe the urban myth that there will be more free time in the summer term, and forget that the combined forces of exam invigilation and planning for next year cancel out any time freed up by absent examination classes.

Nevertheless, if you can spread your burden over a longer period your load may, briefly, be lighter.

Strategy 3 – Spend a weekend catching up

Yes, you will feel very tired on Monday, but balancing that will be a smug sense of satisfaction and the lessening of the load which got you down. You must persevere, set targets, send family away, switch your phone off, take breaks every two hours or so – and most of all *stop* when you're finished. Then resolve to avoid getting into this position again.

Strategy 4 – Practise saying 'no' to more

You may have got into this position because you willingly take on extra work. Now practise saying 'no'. There is no shame in refusing to do more, especially when you are already overloaded. Be realistic about what you can cope with.

Strategy 5 – Prioritize

Often people who say they don't have time for something have simply made it a lower priority than other activities. Prioritizing means deciding quickly how important something is, how imminent is the deadline and what the effects will be if you don't do it.

Maintain a 'To do' list with three main categories: 'Urgent', 'Important' and 'Long term'. Within each category place the item higher or lower according to importance, urgency and consequence. Some personal organizers and some email calendars have features of this kind, though a simple list with space for the three categories will do so long as you don't mind rewriting it from time to time.

Strategy 6 – Regular small doses

Bite-size portions are more digestible than blow-out meals. Ten exercise books every day are less exhausting than 35 at once. Many frequent small actions diminish the effect of the load.

Priorities

Do something – anything!

Alternatives

Work harder. It may be necessary in the short term.

Work smarter. Working smarter involves rationing your energies, prioritizing, being realistic about what you can achieve and aiming for a better work–life balance (which is not a euphemism for laziness).

Revisiting your job description and workload. If there really is a need for an assistant or some extra help, then make out a case for it. Labelling, filing and photocopying might be more effectively done by secretarial staff, or your own son or daughter (in return for pocket money). If you're expected to do too much, discuss with your line manager what you can put on the back burner or abandon altogether.

Avoid

Ignoring the problem. That really will make things worse.

Doing the nearest or easiest thing instead of the most important thing.

Storing up problems which realistically you can't solve.

Lying about the situation. Even small lies about having left something at home or about having 'nearly' finished when you are far from doing so lead to a habit of ignoring the problem and damage your credibility.

7 FILING, STORING, RETRIEVING

I can't find anything and daren't throw anything away!

Description

Every teacher deserves a desk, a laptop, a filing cabinet, basic stationery and tools. If you have an office of your own too, congratulations, you've made it!

Cause

Paperwork piles up because you are not ruthless in throwing it away and not efficient in filing it. Real paper piles up visibly, but electronic information collects at least as much – if not so visibly. Then there are the things you leave at home but find you need while at school – and vice versa.

Action

If you don't have your own desk and space – complain, or just move in.

Designing your filing cabinet.

Preparation is important if filing is going to work, so take time to think about the topics you teach and the headings you'd find useful. Here's a list to start you off:

> pupils, reports, policies, marking, assessment, assemblies, national curriculum, pastoral, working parties, finance, correspondence, instructions and manuals, staffing, governors, union, professional association, timetables, clubs . . .

To this add an in tray, a pending tray, a post tray and a waste-paper basket. You have the beginnings of a system.

Now you can tackle that pile of paper. Label the suspended files for the filing cabinet and look at each set of papers just once. Decide whether to act on it, file it or bin it. Put the 'act on its' in the in tray and create a new file if there is no suitable file available. Don't save stuff just for the sake of it. Ask yourself 'What is the worst that can happen if I bin this?'

Repeat the process regularly and also at the end of each term. Some people come in to school on the first day of the holidays to sort out and tidy up, which provides an opportunity to clean up while the issues of the term are still in your mind. Then you can start afresh next term.

File items at the front of each file so there is some sense of chronology. If the file becomes too big, sort through it, throw away anything unnecessary and divide the file by meaningful topic. So the literature file becomes 'Poetry', 'Plays' and 'Novels' rather than 'Literature' and 'More literature'.

Designing your laptop

Electronically the same basic system can take shape as with your filing cabinet. Identify useful topic headings, create folders and subfolders and save your work.

Ensure you make regular back-ups to another drive or the school server. Then back-up to a DVD now and again and keep that safely at home.

Move resources between home and school on a memory stick or the laptop itself but don't keep the single copy of a file on movable media; make sure there's a second copy somewhere.

Save browser 'Favorites' and make sure they are regularly backed up too.

Keep user names and passwords cunningly disguised or well memorized. Consider a password of no less than six characters made from a favourite song or saying and use the initial letters or sounds ('I'm dreaming of a white Christmas too' becomes 1DOAWX2).

Priorities

The ability to retrieve useful items when required.

Alternatives

Consider storing sets of teaching materials in a common departmental area while retaining the original master copy. Make a visible red dot on the top left-hand corner of each master page – and never give it away.

Keep back-ups of anything you produce yourself.

Avoid

Keeping stuff 'just in case'.

Throwing away unique materials.

Losing everything when your laptop crashes or is stolen.

8 PUPIL ABSENCE

Donna is frequently away and she's falling behind in her studies.

Description

Absence from lessons disrupts a pupil's learning and causes aggravation for teachers. It may be a symptom of illness or of something less obvious, though more significant, in the child's life. At any rate it needs to be recorded and repeated absence or a pattern of absence must be acted upon.

Cause

Real or imagined illness leading to repeated absence requires medical intervention and the school has a duty and a right to check that this is happening.

Pretended illness or other excuses for absence need following up too. Is it fear of something at school? Is it a problem at home such as caring for a young sibling? Is it simple skiving – and if so are there care issues while the child is unsupervised?

Action

First, record the absences. Make sure your records are accurate and clear up any grey areas relating to lateness, approved school visits, medical and dental appointments, etc. Check absence from early registration with absence from lessons throughout the day.

Ensure notes are received from home to explain all the absences.

Keep the notes as evidence, check handwriting and introduce the topic at parents evening.

Phone home for any absence where there is a doubt. Adopt a breezy 'just checking' tone but pay attention to the voice that answers. It is not unknown for the pupil or a sister to answer and pretend to be mother.

Finally, consider involving social services in cases where you suspect the family is covering for the child. Parents are obliged to send their children to school and they have a duty of care in law.

Priorities

Verifying genuine absence and exposing false absence.

Assuring yourself of each child's safety.

Ensuring records of absence for exam candidates are backed up by medical evidence if they are to be used with the exam board.

Alternatives

Propose an absence tracker – an administrative assistant charged with contacting parents on the first day of absence and watching trends.

Use an electronic register to plot patterns of absence.

Avoid

Ignoring the issue or treating it as a low-level problem.

Accepting too many excuses too often without checking.

9 DATA COLLECTION

The Head has asked for more data and I just don't have time to dig it out!

Description

Data on all aspects of education – buildings, systems, pupils, teachers, environmental features ... even sometimes education – is required by government agencies to monitor effectiveness and inform decision-making. It's a valuable practice, but creates difficulties when it comes at busy times and interferes with the very education it's supposed to be checking.

Cause

The data is required in a variety of different formats because those who ask for it have different needs, so data collection and processing can become onerous tasks especially when this seems to land on the school in random, uncoordinated bursts.

Action

Appoint a data collector whose task is to field the requests, gather the data, process it appropriately and send it promptly. If they can then follow up the data by tracking down reports where it appears and make comparisons relative to other schools, this will benefit the school. It is the interpretation of these results which is crucial if it is to benefit the school and an appropriately skilled person can help a Head come to informed decisions.

Some of this data should be collected constantly throughout the school year or come at predictable times. School management systems should be able to collate absence statistics, examination results, etc. with minimum additional intervention. The chief data collector should be able to smooth out the patches of greatest activity by organizing collecting at other times.

Financial software should be able to track aspects of spending and be able to tell whether, say, spending on buildings is increasing over departmental capitation or bin bags and skips over books.

Collecting this data in such a way as to minimize the impact on teachers is important. If you are a Head compelled by others to collect data, don't hesitate to point out to your staff that it is the decision of government, not you. And if you can demonstrate the benefits to the school, emphasize that instead.

Priorities

Generate statistics with minimum pressure on teaching staff to collect it but maximum benefit to the school by interpreting and acting upon it.

Alternatives

Use electronic methods whenever possible. Consider electronic means of recording absences and use examination board data in spreadsheets for its searchability and interpretation.

Do question the organizations which request the data to see if it is useful, necessary or can be collected in a simpler way or from someone else (council, LEA, unions, social or health departments).

Avoid

Spending too much time on trivial counting and measuring tasks which will not benefit the school.

Landing collecting tasks on classroom teachers. If this is unavoidable, emphasize the benefits to the school – assuming there are some . . . .

10 ROOM BOOKING

I planned to use the Resources Centre but there was a confusion over bookings!

Description

Secondary school timetables are designed to fit every class and every teacher into a room, mostly at a regular time for a whole year. Empty rooms may be uneconomical.

In the first week or two any problems will probably be revealed, but after that bookings in common or shared areas like Learning Resources Centre, ICT rooms and sports halls need to be made officially and in advance.

Informal room swaps can work very well, but may have unforeseen timetable effects, (lost children, messages going astray) so inform the timetabler of any changes.

Cause

Double bookings are usually caused by an inefficient booking system. This may include a harassed technician or secretary, a small exercise book or an unclear computer booking interface.

Sometimes overefficiency or selfishness such as booking the television/library/computer room for the whole year in advance when you don't intend to use it can cause trouble too.

Action

Book any room changes as far in advance as practical.

Talk to any teacher who may have (or assume they have) priority to the room you want.

Spontaneous changes may be good creative teaching but they carry with them the risk of failure.

Prepare for failure by always having a back-up plan.

Priorities

Negotiating and talking to people beforehand.

Knowing where you can go if all else fails.

Always have a learning activity that can be carried out anywhere.

Alternatives

In fair weather consider the school grounds. English teachers can do descriptive exercises concentrating on the five senses; Maths teachers can do surveys measuring, counting and calculating litter, wild flowers, traffic, distances of paths and areas of buildings; Science and Geography teachers can count and describe the contents of metre squares (Darwin counted earthworms this way!); Science and PE teachers can also perform aerobic exercises and measure heart rate before and afterwards; Art teachers can draw, paint, collect and create using natural forms or the built environment (tip – investigate textures and forms close up by looking at things only a hand span away).

Some Heads think that leaving the classroom and going outdoors leads to indiscipline and a lack of serious learning. This may be so when it is a novel experience for children normally cooped up in a room, but they will settle with practice.

Consider asking your librarian for some specially selected boxes of books so you can bring the library into your classroom.

Bringing laptops into the classroom instead of moving out to a dedicated computer room offers flexibility and a sense of integration with your other lessons – but do check that it works first!

Avoid

Taking over a room without warning.

Assuming you have rights because you're an older or more experienced teacher.

Arguments in the corridor over who should take the room you want.

Trailing children around the school in search of a spare room.

Getting hot, bothered and angry.

Losing children along the way.

11 VISITORS

Description

Visitors can enhance the curriculum, provide variety, change and a bit of excitement for the class. They are an opportunity which needs to be organized if you are to make the most of them.

Cause

For unexpected visitors see p. 121 above, but look out for traps even for planned visits. Sometimes people from outside schools have different expectations of pupil behaviour or the level of language they need to use.

Action

Be clear beforehand of what you want your visitor to do. If there is a demonstration, do you have space and equipment (good-sized tables and chairs, projector, laptop, screen, electrical socket, blinds . . .)? Is it better out of doors, in a hall or a classroom? Is it safe? Is there a possibility that some children could be frightened/allergic/overexcited by the visitor's presentation/pet/equipment?

Explain to the visitor the topic or purpose, the level of detail required if it is a talk, the age and ability of pupils.

Prepare the children. Discuss appropriate questions, what their task is (beyond simply listening with rapt attention), your expectations of their behaviour.

Arrange and confirm time of arrival, where to sign in, who to contact, how long the session will last.

Decide on whether to offer tea and biscuits in the room, join the staff in the staffroom, share lunch with the children, etc.

Confirm this also with the school secretary so she will expect the visitor and know how to cope, whether to offer tea if the visitor is early, indicate the loos or guide the visitor straight in.

Arrange if possible for one or two children to greet the visitor, guide him/her to your room at the appropriate time and back to the school office.

Prepare other staff for possible delays affecting the next lesson if you overrun or absent pupils if they will miss a lesson. Inform the Head as a matter of courtesy but also in case an informal chat with the Head may be helpful.

Provide clear instructions on how to get to you and phone numbers – yours for advance arrangements, the school's for emergencies and delays.

Ask a child or a group of children to write a thank-you letter following the visit.

For special guests consider a hand-drawn card or a posy of flowers.

Priorities

Timing of arrival and departure to match the timetable and the activity.

If the visitor overruns, be prepared to step in and, politely but firmly, cut the proceedings short. As organizer it is up to you to do so and as long as you have prepared and informed the visitor thoroughly beforehand you should be OK.

Alternatives

Arrange cover for yourself or find a time when you could be free before or after the visit so you are not rushed.

Arrange for someone else to take over as host or hostess if you are committed elsewhere.

Avoid

Overcomplex arrangements.

Too tight timing.

A visitor with a reputation for being difficult.

12 MAKING THE MOST OF TEACHING ASSISTANTS

I have a TA who seems to get in the way instead of helping – yet everyone else says she's great!

Description
A teaching assistant (TA) should be an invaluable aide, not a hindrance. They deserve to be kept informed about what you are teaching, why you are teaching it and how together you might best help pupils benefit from this. It's up to you to talk with the TA.

Cause
Teaching assistants want to help, but few want to take over. That's the job of the teacher. An assistant should not be left in charge of a whole class and the ultimate responsibility for all the pupils is yours. Discussing beforehand how you might help each other is very important and either ignoring or rushing this helps no one.

Action
Compare timetables and book a suitable slot for talking about your plans for the class. Find out how you intend to work together, mutual strengths and weaknesses, issues with individual pupils or small groups.

Prepare your lessons at least as well or better than you would on your own so you can build in plans for both of you.

Take the opportunity of organizing group work or withdrawing individuals for short periods of special attention.

Ask if there are specialized resources you may not know about.

Priorities
Talk to each other beforehand and afterwards. Preparation and evaluation are both important.

Value and respect your TA and show that publicly in front of your pupils.

Emphasize that the pupils must respect the TA as much as you and expect no lower standard of behaviour.

Alternatives
When you are teaching without a TA reflect on how you might have deployed him/her and how some in the class would have benefited.

Avoid
Last minute time-filling activities for your TA.

Loading too much responsibility on your TA.

Treating the withdrawal of a small group with your TA as an embarrassment or a punishment.

13 OUT-OF-SCHOOL VISITS

I'm too terrified to take children out of school – the responsibility is too great!

Description

Learning beyond the school is immensely valuable. Children behave differently in new environments, they learn in different ways and often more intensely than in the relatively predictable classroom. They deserve to be offered lasting educational experiences – yet our litigious society, an obsessive health and safety culture and the amount of organizational effort involved make it so easy simply to stay at school.

Cause

Teachers are right to be wary of taking children on visits and journeys where they have greater responsibility for health and safety and risk being sued for any errors. The best way to overcome this fear is to take every reasonable precaution to avoid known risks and put into place checks and balances to reduce the chances of problems. You *must* be well organized.

This applies to a one-hour traffic survey in the local town, a day out in the city or a four-day visit abroad. In every case you have to ensure the safety of all pupils. Nevertheless there will be different regulations for brief local visits and overnight visits abroad.

Action

First and foremost consult school, union and local authority policies on procedures for school trips. Consider these all carefully before agreeing to take responsibility for an out-of-school visit. Refer to them constantly during your planning.

Follow staffing guidelines for the age and gender of your party. Remember that while parents and governors may count as adults in some circumstances they may not be as responsive or child-orientated as members of staff.

Consider the educational benefits of the visit. Distinguish between an escorted holiday and an educational visit. Both have merits but only a well-prepared, educationally orientated visit deserves to be carried out in school time. That doesn't mean it has to stick rigidly to the National Curriculum, but it does mean it should be both enjoyable and focused on learning.

Consider how the learning can integrate with classroom curriculum work and take advantage of this in preparation and follow-up activities back at school.

Compile a thorough checklist for your specific visit using the official guidelines. Then have it checked by experienced staff or your local authority. Include information about:

> risk assessment, medical issues, travel sickness, travel, transfers, luggage security and transport, local food, insurance, contact information, phone lists, telephone trees, signed parent agreements

and consent to cover responsibilities of both parents and children, preliminary parent and pupil meetings, proposed action in case of disruption by pupils, action and insurance in case of hospitalization or crashes, insurance to cover emergency flights home, staffing ratio to cover your group, competency of any other adults, staff training, first-aid training, a published and agreed itinerary, supervisory arrangements for 24-hour care, worksheets, standards of behaviour, finance and payment, spending money, allowed and recommended equipment and clothing, passports and visas, ski passes, museum tickets, weather conditions, ...

Priorities

Obtain official approval first for your outline of the activity, later for the complete plan with aims, outcomes, itinerary and safety.

Safety.

Follow official advice to the letter.

Cover all foreseeable problems and as many of the unforeseeable ones as you can.

Justify the visit educationally.

Check everything. Then again.

Alternatives

Stay at school and watch a DVD.

Visit websites created by schools who have used their experiences educationally and presented them to benefit others.

Avoid

Complacency.

Fear.

PART 9 PARENTS AND HOME

While we deal every day with children, their parents are also our 'clients'. We shouldn't forget that they may receive a curiously filtered view of our school and our teaching. It is up to us to make sure that parents know what's going on – and hear our point of view.

1 PARENTS EVENINGS

I always seem to overrun at parents evenings. How can I give everyone a fair hearing and keep to schedule?

Description

Parents' consultations (not necessarily in the evening) need a series of time slots.

It's up to you to ensure that you give adequate time to each set of parents, allowing for any problems the child may have, how frequently you see the parents and whether the parents of the child are coming together or separately.

Cause

Parents naturally like to discuss their child at length, while teachers naturally want to make use of limited time and to be fair to all parents. The solution lies in the time allocation.

If you are a secondary-school teacher teaching 100 pupils in a year group, you should be able to deter parents from coming and to some extent select the parents you need to see. Make this clear to pupils well in advance.

If you are a primary teacher most parents will want to see you – indeed any who don't show interest may be the most important ones to contact.

Action

The time slots will normally be agreed by the school, with a beginning and end time and each slot long enough to give time to each child. No time is ever long enough for some parents, so be firm though courteous and work within your 5–15 minute slot.

If, from experience, you find that you consistently overrun or need a breathing space, build in buffers to your time slots.

If you intend to show pupils' work have it methodically laid out in order beforehand. Use it to make a definite educational point rather than simply as window dressing (though that can be worthwhile too).

Priorities

Be courteous and efficient. Don't use being warm and friendly as an excuse for dragging out the time.

Deal with important concerns.

Demonstrate that you know the child and that you care. Developing a good relationship with parents takes time but you may only have minutes.

Alternatives

If it is clear there are too many parents to see in the time available, contact parents explaining why it isn't possible to see everyone. Say you will invite those whose children you are concerned about and suggest to others that where there are real concerns you will speak with them on the phone.

Real concerns need not wait for a formal parents evening and should be dealt with quickly. This is also true of concerns which emerge as a result of the consultation. Note these and act on them.

Avoid

Spending too long with verbose parents at the expense of parents who have real concerns.

Sighing with relief that it's over and ignoring the real concerns which emerge from the meeting.

2 WHAT TO SAY AND WHAT NOT TO SAY

I'm afraid of putting my foot in it and saying the wrong thing!

Description

You may talk to a large number of people in a short space of time and you need to represent yourself, your school and your profession in the best possible way.

Cause

For you, each parent is one among many, but for them it may be the only time they have personal contact with you and the school for the whole year. They are often intent on memorizing or noting down what you say about their child so they can report back, so every word you say counts.

Action

Have your notes, assessment records and marked work or portfolios available and in accessible order. If you're short of time don't refer to exercise books; summarize work quality instead.

Treat the evening as a practice run for a written report and have all your material at hand.

Employ euphemisms rather than describing a pupil as stupid, evil or deranged. Even if it's true.

If you are a secondary-school teacher with large numbers of pupils, discreetly employ a photograph of the child to check identity.

Priorities

Say what you can based on evidence.

Say positive things where possible but don't shy away from honest criticism based on behaviour and performance.

Alternatives

If you are a secondary-school teacher teaching an able and charming pupil, don't be afraid to stun the parents at the very beginning with wholehearted praise for them and their child and direct them on their way without more ado: 'Mr and Mrs Taylor, I'd just like to say how fortunate you are to have such a charming, hard-working and able daughter. She has done well, will continue to do well and is a pleasure to teach. Thank you and goodbye!'

Avoid

Turgid conversations with parents who think their children are far brighter than they really are.

Drawing out any conversation beyond the limits of the information you have available, unless you really do have lots of time to spare.

3 RESPONDING TO PARENTAL REQUESTS

The mother of a girl in my class worries about her and sends me notes. What should I do?

Description

Notes from parents can sometimes seem intrusive, but they may also show they care.

Cause

Reasons for sending messages to the teacher may lie anywhere on the spectrum from obsessive clinging to furious anger – with themselves, their child or you. Most parents do care, and feel that an answer to a question or knowing that you are aware of a potential problem will help their child's education.

Action

Action will depend on your knowledge of the parent, the child, the number of previous notes and the complexity of the question or comment.

Make a quick judgement about the importance of the note. If it seems straightforward, acknowledge receipt either by jotting a note in the child's day book/homework book or by adding a thanks and signature to the note itself. If you're lucky enough to have a headed compliments slip, sign that and add a few words indicating all is well.

If the note indicates potential illness or the possibility that the child may be upset because of the death of a pet or relative, deal with this quickly and considerately, showing the child you care but not overdoing the sympathy or compounding the trauma. Just make sure you don't have the class write about their favourite pets . . . .

Excuses for work not done should be dealt with appropriately and firmly, emphasizing that this should not recur and that the work must be done as soon as possible.

Administrative tasks such as payment for a trip or giving a holiday permission form may be best done by sending the child to the school office without your intervention.

More important messages, long letters of complaint, concern about the child's general education or some other teacher's dealings with the child will require more thought than you can give at the moment. Acknowledge receipt and make clear that you are treating the issue seriously and therefore want to spend time discussing the issue with colleagues.

Important letters like this will deserve more of your time, whether they seem to be baseless or not. The fact is that the parent is expressing concern and you need to find out why. Try to rationalize it and see it from the parental point of view rather than blindly supporting your colleagues and your school.

Make sure any relevant concerns are passed on to other colleagues, especially pastoral tutors.

Priorities

Acknowledge receipt of all messages promptly. If necessary, create a pile of acknowledgement slips and keep them to hand.

Decide what is trivial and easily dealt with and what is serious and needs time and thought.

For serious or potentially serious items consult others and look at the problem from all points of view. If it involves other colleagues, consult them for their point of view. If it involves whole school issues, consult the Head or relevant post holder. Determine the facts as far as possible. Keep a note of all written correspondence and avoid phone calls.

Serious issues will require personal meetings, with parents and other colleagues. If there is direct or implicit criticism of you, consider having witnesses to support you. Anything with legal implications deserves help from a professional friend or a union representative. At best this could prevent the issue spiralling out of control. Apologies may be helpful and can defuse the problem, especially at an early stage, but can be seen as an admission of guilt – which can pose problems later.

Alternatives

In primary schools or if you know the parent well enough, answer the question face to face. Sometimes a smile as you say, 'No need to worry, he/she was fine today', will be far more effective than any written note, though written confirmation can be reassuring too.

Avoid

Automatic and thoughtless support of school and teachers against parents.

Assuming that what parents think happened did happen.

Criticizing colleagues in public, except in extreme circumstances.

Contacts

ACAS (Advisory, Conciliation and Arbitration Service)
www.acas.org.uk
Allergy in Schools
www.allergyinschools.org.uk/
Asthma
www.asthma.org.uk/
ATL (Association of Teachers and Lecturers)
www.atl.org.uk
Behaviour4learning
www.behaviour4learning.ac.uk/
British Board of Film Classification
www.bbfc.co.uk/general/index.php
British Dyslexia Association
www.bdadyslexia.org.uk/
BMJ 'Best Treatments' clinical evidence for patients
www.besttreatments.co.uk/btuk/conditions/10236.html
Bully Online
www.bullyonline.org/workbully/teachers.htm
Bureaucracy-cutting toolkit
www.teachernet.gov.uk/wholeschool/remodelling/cuttingburdens/toolkit/
Cambridgeshire Education Portal
www.ccceducation.net
Childline
www.childline.org.uk/
Children's British Board of Film Classification – a young person's guide
www.cbbfc.co.uk/
Commission for Racial Equality
www.cre.gov.uk
Department of Trade and Industry: Employment Matters
www.dti.gov.uk/employment/index.html
Disability Rights Commission
www.drc.org.uk
Dyspraxia Foundation
www.dyspraxiafoundation.org.uk/
Dyspraxia – How ICT benefits students with Dyspraxia
www.ncte.ie/SpecialNeedsICT/TechnologyAdvice/AdviceSheets/Dyspraxia/

Employment Matters (Department of Trade and Industry)
www.dti.gov.uk/employment/index.html
Epilepsy Foundation
www.epilepsy.org.uk/
Equal Opportunities Commission
www.eoc.org.uk
Excellence in Cities Initiative
www.standards.dfes.gov.uk/giftedandtalented/
General Teaching Council (GTC)
Code of Conduct and Practice for Registered Teachers
www.gtce.org.uk/shared/contentlibs/92511/92601/conductcode.pdf
General Teaching Council for Scotland
Professionalism in Practice leaflet
www.gtcs.org.uk
Gifted and Talented – Guidance on teaching the Gifted and Talented
www.nc.uk.net/gt/
Learning Difficulties: Planning teaching and assessing pupils with learning
 difficulties
www.nc.uk.net/ld/
NAS/UWT (The National Association of Schoolmasters/Union of Women
 Teachers)
www.nasuwt.org.uk/
National Remodelling Team (NRT)
www.remodelling.org
NUT (National Union of Teachers)
www.teachers.org.uk/
OFSTED Handbooks for inspecting schools
www.ofsted.gov.uk/inspectors/
Panic Attacks
www.panic-attacks.co.uk/
'Professionalism in Practice' by the General Teaching Council for Scotland
www.gtcs.org.uk/conduct
Stress – UK National Work-Stress Network
www.workstress.net/causes.htm

References

ACAS advice leaflet: Bullying and harassment at work www.acas.org.uk/
 index.aspx?articleid=794Is, accessed 7 December 2006

BMJ *'Best Treatments' clinical evidence for patients* www.besttreatments.co.uk/
 btuk/conditions/10236.html, accessed 7 December 2006

Cambridgeshire County Council (2006) *Managing Bereavement in Cambridgeshire
 Schools.* Cambridgeshire County Council Office of Young People and
 Children's Services

DfES (1998) Circular number 10/98 – Section 550A of the Education Act 1996:
 The Use of Force to Control or Restrain Pupils, HMSO; published online
 at www.dfes.gov.uk/publications/guidanceonthelaw/10_98/part2.htm

Gardner, H. and Hatch, T. (1989) 'Multiple intelligences go to school: Educational implications of the theory of multiple intelligences', *Educational Researcher* 18 (8) 4–9

General Teaching Council for Scotland, 'Professionalism in Practice', Code of Conduct and Practice for Registered Teachers, leaflet obtainable from The General Teaching Council for Scotland, Clerwood House, 96 Clermiston Road, Edinburgh EH12 6UT. Tel: 0131 314 6000; www.gtcs.org.uk/professionalconduct/, accessed 7 December 2006

Grey, D. (2005) *100+ Lists for Teachers*. London, Continuum

NAS/UWT (1996) 'No Place to Hide: Confronting Workplace Bullies', NASUWT Teachers' Union Report April 1996. NASUWT, Hills-Court Education Centre, Rose Hill, Rednal, Birmingham B45 8R5

OFSTED, *Handbook for inspecting secondary schools* (reference code HMI 1360/0113501161); quoted at www.askatl.org.uk under Help and Advice (The Association of Teachers and Lecturers), accessed 7 December 2006

Smith, A. and Call, N. (1999) *The ALPS approach (accelerated learning in primary schools)*. Stafford, Network Educational Press Ltd; available from: www.standards.dfes.gov.uk/thinkingskills/resources/565198, accessed 7 December 2006

Steer Report (2005) *Learning behaviour – The Report of The Practitioners' Group on School Behaviour and Discipline*. Chair: Sir Alan Steer. DFES-1950-2005

The Education (School Teachers' Pay and Conditions) (No. 2) Order 2003, ISBN 0110473949, The Stationery Office

www.gtcs.org.uk/nmsruntime/saveasdialog.asp?lID=255&sID=590

not accessed because of virus warning